HOPE THIS INS

MAKE 'SOMED

EXPERIENTIAL BILLIONAIRE

Experiential Billionaire

BUILD A LIFE RICH IN EXPERIENCES AND DIE WITH NO REGRETS

BRIDGET HILTON & JOE HUFF

EXPERIENTIAL BILLIONAIRE
Build A Life Rich in Experiences and Die With No Regrets
First Edition

ISBN 979-8-9888374-2-8 *Hardcover*
979-8-9888374-1-1 *Paperback*
979-8-9888374-0-4 *Ebook*

*This book is dedicated to Yasmine,
Kai, Kilian, and Taco-Bear.*

*Their unconditional love has given us the
greatest experiences life has to offer.*

Greenland shark, chicken sashimi, live octopus, and actual guinea pigs. (I could keep going, but I don't want PETA to slash my tires. Thankfully, I've yet to see an "ethical treatment of tarantulas" group.) And we've surfed, skateboarded, biked, hiked, fallen down, and gotten lost exploring new places more times than we can count.

Our experiences weren't just about us, though. Along the way, we've helped build schools in Guatemala, installed water filtration systems in Haiti, worked with victims of human trafficking in Indonesia, planted trees all over the US, given hearing aids to people in need all over the world, and helped others achieve their own goals, dreams, and experiences.

We've had tons of fun, but there has also been fear, failure, embarrassment, discomfort, and struggle. Not every experience was pleasant and easy. In fact, the most valuable ones rarely were—that's what made them so transformative. Some of our most rewarding experiences were the ones that didn't work out the way we had planned. And luckily, our happiness was not correlated to our finances—many of our best experiences happened during our worst times financially.

If that's how we felt, how did other people feel? How could we learn from other people's successes and mistakes? We started asking our friends and family questions like, "What were the most valuable experiences of your life? What are your biggest regrets?"

That led to us visiting retirement homes and having conversations with elderly people. Who better to share their wisdom and reflections from their time here on Earth? The experience was both moving and bittersweet, because the heartfelt stories we were told only served to confirm our thesis that regrets grow larger as time grows shorter. It inspired us to go bigger and conduct one of the largest surveys ever done on life experiences, with more than 20,000 participants of all ages from around the world.

What we found were clear patterns that led some people to become what we call experiential billionaires, while others wound up experientially bankrupt—and out of time. To write this book, we took those patterns and put them into actionable steps to break through the barriers to have the experiences we wanted most in life, such as gorilla trekking in Rwanda...which ended like this:

Twenty-four hours after our harrowing drive up the mountain in a tropical storm, we came face to face with a different kind of natural phenomenon. Well, face to ground actually. If we looked up at the wrong moment, there was a decent chance we could get our faces ripped off by a 400-pound silverback gorilla. Those were the warnings of Charles and François, whose lives were devoted to keeping these wild and amazing creatures safe from poachers. The gorillas might have taken direct eye contact as a threat, and there were babies to protect—extremely adorable babies that I had to hold myself back from cuddling.

We stared in wonder as they made the hillside into their never-ending playground, tumbling, spinning, climbing, and rolling around, as toddlers do—just a few feet from us.

PART I

Make Your Treasure Map

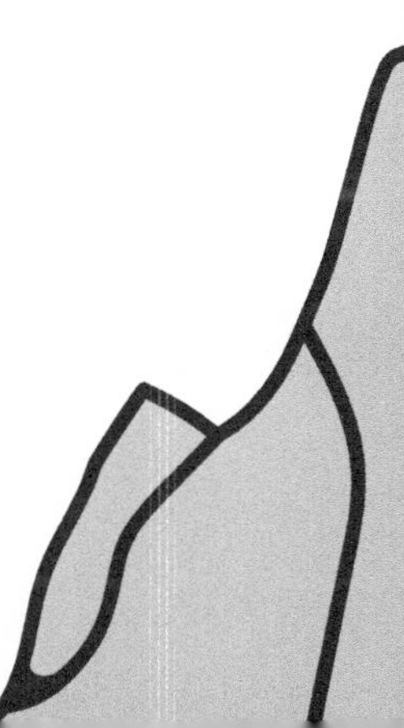

Chapter One

YOU KNOW HOW THIS ENDS

"Twenty years from now you will be more disappointed by the things that you didn't do than by the ones you did do."

—Mark Twain

Joe:

What's the best place to start when you are about to embark on the path to the most rich and rewarding life possible? The very end.

When we are born, we are all diagnosed with the same condition: death. It's inevitable. You are going to die. Yes, I mean *you*.

I know what you're thinking: *Yeah, I know. So glad I bought a book to tell me that*. But do you *really know?*

Most people bury this knowledge in the back of their brains and heap on distraction upon distraction—anything to avoid seriously reflecting on the fact that our time here is limited. We hide it away in hospitals and retirement homes. We pay lip service with bumper-sticker phrases like "life is short" or "you only live once," but mostly we just suppress thoughts of our own mortality.

Bringing up this topic is considered bad form. Society operates under a silent agreement to keep any mention of our mortality off-limits. And when it happens—a friend gets in a car accident, a relative passes from a heart attack—you still might think, *That's not going to happen to me*.

Well, unfortunately, life is not a dress rehearsal, and death is too important to ignore. To embrace and understand what it means to really live, we need to make sure our relationship with and understanding of death is honest and realistic.

Fear of death is natural and even healthy. After all, that fear helps keep you out of harm's way. What's problematic is the fear of *contemplating* death. Paradoxically, if you never think or talk about death, you could end up wasting your life. You could lull yourself into believing you can wait to start living your actual life at some indefinite point in the future...that may never come.

When the end of your life arrives, will you look back at an incredible life story, knowing you lived your one existence to the fullest? Or will you be full of pain and regret because you never made time for the things that mattered to you? If you never face your mortality, you can bet on the latter.

Thinking about your own demise may seem morbid, but in reality, it's the secret to transforming your life. The harshness of death brings a beautiful clarity to life as it should be lived. That's why so many people who have near-death experiences are the ones who change their lives. They wake up with a new sense of urgency. They take that trip. They propose to that girl they love. They run that marathon. They get up early to watch magical sunrises.

We all need to have this urgency—*without* the actual near-death experience.

The Harsh Reality

At age 18, I watched my father's life come to what looked to be a sudden and very early end.

My dad had a tough childhood—growing up with five siblings in a working-class Chicago neighborhood will do that. He met my mom while they were both working on an assembly line making brake pads. He was a notoriously hard worker, the kind of guy who left for work every day at 5 a.m. and didn't get back home until well into the evening. He never complained, though. He was just grateful for life, having witnessed unspeakable things during the Vietnam War, like so many other men from his generation.

Unfortunately, another gift from the war was chronically high blood pressure from Agent Orange exposure. After our family moved to California, he began experiencing other worrying health symptoms as I entered high school. The doctors kept telling him it was simply an ulcer, or some other minor malady that was far from life-threatening. So, Dad plowed ahead with his busy schedule and long hours.

That all ended the morning I came down to discover him slumped at the kitchen table, white as a sheet and drenched in sweat. I called 911 and sat there waiting, helpless, until the paramedics showed up. He was rushed to the hospital to begin what would become a living nightmare that lasted over two months.

My dad didn't have an ulcer—it was a dire case of undiagnosed cardiomyopathy, or swelling and scarring of the heart. His condition was so grave that he was immediately added to the top of the heart transplant list—odds of survival: less than 10 percent.

Grateful as we were for the chance at a transplant, the wait was grueling. Just two weeks in, he had to be resuscitated with defibrillators for the first of what would be several times—a cool scene in a TV medical drama, but an incredibly painful procedure in real life, especially for someone already so frail. It was so bad that he asked not to be resuscitated again.

His heart held on for the next few weeks, even as he lost 40 pounds and became comatose. That's when the doctor pulled us aside to clarify his directive. If he went into cardiac arrest again, we could overrule his choice in the hopes that a transplant would happen soon and dramatically increase his quality of life. We said yes. They pumped one thousand volts into him one more time the very next week.

Time seemed to stop while we waited for a miracle. As we paced the halls, it felt horrible to think this was how so many people lived, eking out vacations and waiting on a retirement they might never see. Postponing life now for a future that might not exist.

As the situation dragged on, I had lots of time to reflect. I was just coming out of a difficult adolescence, complete with a terrifying drug addiction that had peaked with me getting kicked out of high school. Having somehow started to turn my life around, I had been hoping for a victory lap.

Instead, I was shattered to my core and questioning the harsh realities of life as I watched my dad inch painfully toward death at age 50. He had worked so hard his whole life. He got a few vacations out of it, but what else? He had provided for his family, and that certainly wasn't nothing, but still...was this all there was to adult life? Work like crazy, steal a few moments of happiness here and there, and then you're dead?

The more I turned it over in my head, the more upsetting it was. In the end, I could only come to one conclusion: *This. Is. Bullshit.*

No One Knows Their Deadline

The health situation with my dad may not have been avoidable. What was avoidable was the regret he felt about the many things he hadn't done yet because he thought he would have more time.

How many people are going through this same situation right now? How many people just suddenly found out they're out of time? That all the things they planned on doing someday would never happen?

What would you do? How would you feel? Would you try to start planning things you had always wanted to do now that you have a deadline?

Time constraints can work magic for getting to the truth and finding focus. Cramming for midterms. Pulling an all-nighter before a big meeting. Getting your taxes done on April 14th. We all know how a deadline can motivate us to get the important things done...but only if it's specific and feels urgent.

This isn't tax day. This isn't the night before a midterm. This is your life, and it's happening *right now*, whether you're asleep at the wheel or not. You can't just cram it all in at the end and hope for the best.

So, let's stop procrastinating. Here's a thought experiment that will help you start putting things in perspective.

At the end of the chapter, we'll dig in deeper and write it down, but for now, just follow along in your head.

Imagine your doctor just called. He says he got your test results back, and you better sit down: you only have one year left to live. Take a deep breath and let that sink in. Suddenly, your time is finite. Well, it always has been, but now it *feels* finite, like uncountable mounds of cash becoming one wallet full of bills. You can hold it in your hand. You can wrap your head around it.

How will you spend that one year? What are the top 10 things you want to do before time runs out?

Now ask yourself this: how many of those 10 things are you actively working toward now?

If you're like most people, the answer is none. That's what research has found, including our own global *Life Experience Survey*.

It turns out, most people—76 percent per Cornell, over 80 percent in our survey—regret the things they haven't done far more than the ones they have. The goals they had never achieved or even tried to achieve. The places they had always wanted to go but never went. The things they had always wanted to learn but never made time for. In our survey, participants told us they always wanted to go to Italy, climb a mountain, learn Spanish, start a nonprofit, learn to play guitar, and so much more.

Why do so many of us give up on having the experiences that we know will bring us so much value in life? Well, that's the next question we asked.

For 94 percent of the respondents, the reason was one variation or another of "I just never got around to it."

It sounds crazy, but it makes sense. We aren't taught to prioritize seeking out and investing in new experiences. When we're kids, we don't go to school to learn how to live a fulfilling life and pursue our dreams. We don't realize that our experiences are the only things in life that we can never lose. No one tells us having more experiences will make us healthier and live longer. And what could be more valuable than that?

So, what does value even mean? Just do a quick search on Google for "valuable." You'll see sparkling diamonds, some weird gold eggs, and toilet paper made from hundred-dollar bills (try it and see for yourself). Yet, when we asked actual human beings in our study what the most valuable things in their lives were, none of the 20,000+ respondents clutched their pearls and answered with "my brick of gold," "my Rolls Royce," or "my diamond grill." In fact, the vast majority of respondents *didn't include anything financial or material at all.*

Still, we make excuses and postpone our personal goals. We tell ourselves the lie that we'll eventually get around to it. And then we keep putting them off...until it's too late.

Well, hopefully your doctor didn't just call you and tell you you're dying in 12 months. It would be pretty weird if they knew that exact timeline anyway, and we're sure they would be running a very in-demand practice if they did.

We need to confront death, but without the necessity of a dramatic, life-threatening situation. We need a way to force death into our consciousness and honestly reflect on the finiteness of life. That might sound a bit masochistic, but it's not at all. It's actually a way to jolt you onto a new path—one guided by intentionality and urgency—so you begin having the life experiences you truly desire.

A great way to inspire some urgency is a Memento Mori chart. "Memento Mori" is a phrase that has served as a call to arms for centuries and translates to "remember you must die."

THE AVERAGE HUMAN LIFESPAN IN YEARS

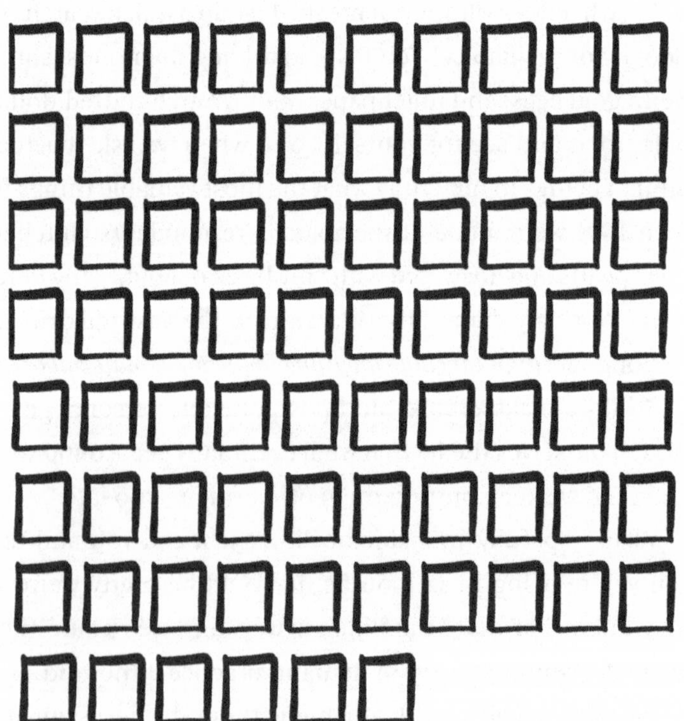

Download available at ExperientialBillionaire.com.

The chart makes that concept visual. It has 76 boxes, one for each year of the average American lifespan. Fill in the boxes for the years you've already lived. What remains is the years you have left to live—and a powerful reminder that life is finite. It might be off-putting or even scary...but isn't it even scarier to think you could ignore this reality and let your life slip away?

So, scary as it may seem, put the chart up on your wall. Take a picture of it and make it your phone background. Do *something* so you see it every day and feel time constantly ticking. You need that urgency—it pushes you to make the most of your time.

On top of creating urgency, the Memento Mori chart also prompts you to consider the math of your life experiences (assuming an average lifespan, of course).

For example, let's say you're 40 years old, so in theory you have 36 years left. How many times do you travel for leisure each year? Is it only once? Okay, then you better pick the 36 places you want to see before you die. Oh yeah, don't forget that you'll probably want to go some places more than once, and by the time you're almost 80, you likely won't be globe-trotting (kudos if so, though!). With this math, maybe you'll see 15 or 20 more places in your remaining 36 years.

Have little ones in your life? Say your child is nine right now, which means you have nine more summers with them until they're old enough to move out of the house. If you want to do that great American family road trip, now is the time to plan it.

What about your parents? How many blocks are filled out on their Memento Mori? Let's say they are 65 years old, so they have 11 more blocks on the chart. How many times do you see them a year? Multiply that by 11 and that's how many more times you'll see them in your life. Seems more urgent than you thought, doesn't it?

Life 2.0

Back to St. Vincent's Medical Center. After 70 days of waiting for a heart, my family watched as a helicopter landed on the hospital roof, bearing the heart of a 23-year-old man who had died in a motorcycle accident only an hour or two earlier. It was overwhelming and surreal to see what looked like an ordinary red Igloo cooler being carried off the helicopter, knowing that instead of beers for a backyard BBQ, it actually held the heart of someone whose own sudden and tragic death would give my dad a second chance at life.

The next few weeks were a blur. The surgery went well, and the recovery was a roller coaster, but eventually the transplant was deemed successful. Then it was just a waiting game—waiting for the dramatic improvement in quality of life the doctors had promised.

It didn't materialize. Dad remained weak and hospitalized for two more months, and when he was finally discharged, he moved with his brother into an apartment close to the hospital, in case he needed emergency care. Even out of the hospital, he was sick all the time and remained exceptionally frail. When I asked him if he was glad we had resuscitated him, he looked at me from the sunken hole in the sofa, as he sat in his faded dark blue sweatpants that smelled of hospital, a gray stubble on his chin and an even grayer pallor on his face, and said "no" without missing a beat. Clearly things weren't turning out as we had hoped.

As the misery continued, my uncle, also a Vietnam vet, was himself diagnosed with cardiomyopathy and put on permanent disability (he would soon wind up with a heart transplant himself). He looked at my dad and decided enough was enough. He suggested they move out of that tiny, depressing apartment in the city and go live somewhere more relaxing—close to the water, within driving distance of family. With a combined fixed income of just $1,600 a month, that could only mean one thing: Mexico.

My dad reached out to me for advice, and I didn't hesitate. "You should go," I told him. His doctors were very concerned. They called me directly and listed all the risks and reasons why he absolutely shouldn't go, but my brothers and I discussed it and we knew we'd rather see our dad live one week enjoying the beach in Mexico than years visiting an endless procession of doctors in Riverside, California. We wanted him to live a life, not be kept alive. He had nothing to lose.

They packed up the car and drove down the coast, aiming vaguely for Zihuatanejo. Their only reference was the movie *Shawshank Redemption*, where Zihautanejo was the location of the happy ending for the two men who had been sentenced to life in prison. Fitting indeed. They themselves had been sentenced to a life they refused to accept, so just like the characters in the movie, they escaped. They never quite made it that far south, but they did stumble upon a magical beach town called San Carlos. They found a little beachfront house for $400 a month and signed a six-month lease.

They settled there "temporarily," hoping to use it as a base to figure out where they might eventually live in Mexico—and then a small miracle happened. In just a few weeks, my dad's health showed a remarkable improvement. His doctors, who had advised against the trip, were now speculating that leaving behind the stressful orbit of the hospital had created a turning point.

For the rest of us, it was crystal clear. He was thriving in his new environment. He knew he wasn't going to waste his life this time around.

He surrounded himself with the colorful characters that often are the signature of small beach towns in remote areas of the world. He took a totally new approach to life, filling it with joyful experiences he had never made time for in the past. Spearfishing, sailing, hiking, mountain biking—Dad did it all.

Before his transplant, he hadn't made time for many friends or social experiences. On my first visit, I was surprised to find that he had already become a much-loved local in town and had forged some wonderful friendships with a wide and wild variety of people.

Having the only phone with long-distance service, he invited all of his expat friends to come make calls when needed. They quickly started to congregate at his house throughout the day, where they would log their calls home on a sheet of paper so they could pay him when the bill came.

He used those inevitable daily gatherings as an excuse to start what he called the "Isuzu drinking club" (he drove an Isuzu Trooper at the time). The only club rule? "You don't really have to own an Isuzu." Those daily gatherings almost always devolved into a chess tournament, a kayaking trip, a sunset dinner, or some other fun activity. Eventually, the town got more infrastructure and his friends got their own phone lines, but the gatherings and adventures continued unabated.

It was a joyful time, watching him fill up his agenda with experiences, surrounded by such a close-knit community of friends.

The Gift of Urgency

His second life made a huge impression on me. He could have done the "safe" thing and stayed stuck in the apartment in Riverside, clinging in fear to the shadow of the hospital. But to transform, we need to leave our safety behind. So, instead, he made a decision to change and built a new life loaded with the things he wanted to do most.

My dad's ordeal gave me a great gift: *urgency*. I was suddenly very aware that there wasn't a guarantee on how much time I had to experience my dreams and fulfill my goals. As a result, while my dad started off on his bonus round (as he liked to call it), I started trying to figure out how to do all the things I wanted to do.

Of course, I still had the same problems as before—problems that most people have. Sure, I had some vague desires, but I didn't know where to start. I had no connections. I didn't have much money. And most importantly, I hadn't put time into figuring out what my dreams even were.

But with my newfound sense of urgency, I started making lists of things I wanted to do—and actually *doing* them.

I'd always wanted to try stand-up comedy. It seemed terrifying, but I realized if I didn't do it now, I might never, so I went for it. Living on my own, I missed my mom's cooking, so I pulled out some old cookbooks and started learning some of my favorite family recipes. I saved up for a couple months and went skydiving with three of my best friends. I volunteered at a soup kitchen for Thanksgiving. Things that I knew I'd regret if I reached the end of my life without doing them. Things that didn't take much time or money, just urgency and intention.

I identified some adventures that I didn't know whether I would enjoy or not, but I wanted to at least try them. I went cliff diving (loved it), free diving (super cool), and long-distance cycling (learned that, although I love riding bikes, my butt has a time limit on a bike seat). Achieving those types of goals gave me great personal satisfaction and added value to my life immediately.

But my life still seriously lacked direction. I was struggling to find opportunities for both financial and personal growth. Spending my high school years on drugs instead of planning for a future had left me with few role models to look up to. Most of the friends I grew up with were struggling to transition into adulthood, with many still battling addiction. A few went to jail. A few died. Then a few more.

I didn't know what I wanted—but I knew it wasn't that.

I wanted to get out and start somewhere new. Somewhere I could have a clean slate and hopefully find a group of like-minded people who wanted more. But where?

By chance, I went to a friend's house for a small gathering. He introduced me to two of his girlfriends from a neighboring high school. We got to talking and they started telling me how they wanted to move to Newport Beach. "Move to the beach? That sounds amazing!" I said, with the fantasy of living in board shorts and flip flops in my head. Growing up, I had always wanted to learn how to surf, but my parents, being originally from Chicago, rarely took our family to the beach, even though it was only about 45 minutes away.

I told them I would move with them and they laughed and said, "That sounds great! We'd love to have a guy roommate!" We exchanged phone numbers and went home. After a night of typical underage drinking, it was safe to assume we had all been just joking around.

But when I got home, the thought percolated until I couldn't stop thinking about it. I thought about all the times my friends and I had talked about moving to the beach when we "grew up." When was that going to be? When I moved out, why had I moved to a town I had no reason to live in, so close to home? What was I clinging to? I started thinking about all the excuses my friends would most likely make about why we didn't move to the beach like we had said we'd do.

The urgency in me screamed, "Why not *now*?"

I spent the next few weeks searching for places and calling dozens of potential landlords. Initially, I thought there were a lot of great options, but I quickly discovered many of those options required credit history (weird, I know) or were looking for a family (oddly, a lot of landlords don't want to rent their homes to three 19-year-olds). I plowed forward with the little time I had between the two jobs I was working—the glamorous night shift at a factory making tractor trailer truck sidings and daytime quality control inspections at random job sites.

I finally found the perfect place, an affordable three-bedroom house only one block from the beach. The owners were cool and said I was the first person to call, so if I could send in our application and a security deposit, the place was ours. "No problem!" I said. Now I just had to call the girls and tell them—and hope they had been serious or were at least open to the idea.

"Hey! Remember me? Well, have you moved to the beach yet? No? Great, because I found a place and I think it's perfect."

Two weeks later, I moved to the beach with two girls I met at a party.

The Stakes Are High

A little over a decade after moving to Mexico, my dad got cancer, likely as a side effect from the immunosuppressant drugs that are part of the transplant process. He fought the cancer successfully once, but when it returned a second time, it couldn't be beat. He ended up being airlifted to the Veterans Administration hospital in Tucson, Arizona, and I went there to stay with him as he "circled the drain" (those are his words—even at the very end, he never lost his sense of humor).

He still had dreams of somehow beating the cancer, and his wife prayed day and night as well, but we found in-home hospice care for him all the same. Slowly, he wound down until he finally became more or less comatose for most of the day, only waking to request more morphine for the pain. We called his family and friends to let them know that if they wanted to see him again, now was the time.

Luckily, his two best friends from San Carlos were able to come. As soon as they arrived, he came alive again, and, for a miraculous two hours, I watched them reminisce about all the wonderful times they had had together. They talked about the sailing, the Thanksgiving dinners, the car crashes, the unsettled bar tabs (and bar fights), the live music, the moonlight swims, the hikes through the desert, and the charity they had started with $100 each, which had by then raised over $100k and had sent dozens of underprivileged kids to college.

They had always enjoyed giving each other a hard time, and even with my dad's frail state, they never let up. In fact, they went harder than ever—and laughed harder than ever too. The stakes were high and they all knew it. This was my dad's last game. His final bow.

The light that had disappeared from my dad's eyes returned as they remembered stories and jokes. For hours, the long, joyous belly laughs coming from the room sounded as if they were back at the Soggy Peso beach bar, sitting on cheap plastic chairs with their toes in the sand, a fresh round of rum and cokes in front of them, the ocean sunset in the background, and not a care in the world. You would have never known it was a farewell party for their dearest friend. Eventually, it was time for goodbyes, and everyone parted.

They went home and back to their lives. My dad died later that night, but at the very end, I truly believe he rested easier knowing he had amassed a treasure trove of meaningful experiences with people he had loved over the last decade. I'd like to think that was somehow proof he wasn't one of those people who, when it came time to pay the final bill, regretted all the things they hadn't done. But I'll settle for knowing he had a pretty kick ass time in his bonus round of life—and that alone is proof enough for me to believe in the value of a life rich in experiences.

Most people aren't lucky enough to have a near-death experience to show them that "someday" can actually be today. I used to imagine—as many people do—that I would die peacefully in my bed at age 100. I know better now. In reality, few people get to end life that way. Most get far less time and spend far too much of it suffering from painful and debilitating health conditions. And over 14 percent of deaths are completely unexpected, leaving behind countless things left unsaid, unfinished, or never started.[6]

Don't worry, this book isn't one long rant about how you need to hurry up and live before you die. But the urgency you're cultivating now is the motivating force behind everything that follows—practical strategies for building your experiential wealth so you can die without (or at least with way less) regrets, just like my dad.

So, let your new relationship with death be the turning point in your life, when you go from putting off your dreams to actively planning them. The clock is ticking.

✦ ✦ ✦

EXERCISE

Make Your Treasure Map

Don't skip this exercise! It's the cornerstone of your experience-rich life because it helps you identify what you truly value—your experiential treasure. Without that clarity, you could easily just bob around in the ocean of life, at the whims of the tides and winds, never doing what you actually want. We first tested this exercise on ourselves over a decade ago, and since then we've done it with many other people, and we've never seen it fail to produce powerful results.

Before you start, know that this exercise can stir up deep emotions. Let that happen. It means you are getting to the core of how you want to live. In fact, if you're not feeling much at all, you probably aren't digging deep enough yet.

Remember that creepy doctor who called and made you think about how much time you have left? That's actually the beginning of this exercise.

Set aside about 30 to 60 minutes of quiet time, and make sure you're in a place where you won't be interrupted. All you need is an ordinary sheet of paper and a pen.

1. Fold the sheet of paper into thirds to create three columns. In the first column, write "One Year" at the top, then list the top ten things you would want to experience if you only had one year left to live. Give this some real thought, and only list things you could realistically do within the one-year timeframe.

2. In the middle column, do the same for one month. If you only had one month left to live, what are the top ten things you would want to experience? Some overlap with your One Year column is fine. Again, take the time to think deeply, and be realistic.

3. The third column is for one day. What would you do if you had just *one day* left to live? If you knew it was your *final* day?

4. Look at all three lists. How many of those things are you actively working toward now? Put an asterisk next to those things. Alarming, we know.

5. Look at everything that doesn't have an asterisk and ask yourself why. How can something be so important that it's on this list and yet not important enough to do while you still have time? What is stopping you from doing these things now? What barriers (or excuses) have prevented you from doing those things? Time? Money? Fear? Simple lack of initiative? Keep those obstacles in mind because we'll address them in Part II of this book.

6. With the three lists completed, look for patterns. How many experiences overlap and appear in all three columns? That's a flashing red light saying these are what you value the most and should be your top priorities going forward.

Hang onto your Treasure Map; we'll keep using it throughout the book. Post it in a place (like your fridge or mirror) where you'll see it every day. These things matter. These things are your future. Seeing them daily is important—it reminds you of your priorities and helps hold you accountable.

Note: Go to ExperientialBillionaire.com *to download or print an extended version of this exercise in addition to free experience guides.*

Chapter Two

ENVISION YOUR RICH LIFE

"I wanted to live
deep and suck out
all the marrow of life,
to cut a broad swath
and shave close,
to drive life into a
corner, and reduce it
to its lowest terms."

—Henry David Thoreau

Bridget:

I didn't judge anyone who didn't want out of Flint, Michigan, but I knew I was going to find my personal eject button or die trying. As a kid in a small, blue-collar town full of hardworking people, grappling with its fair share of addictions, crime, and harsh economic realities, I fell in love with music and a dream of Hollywood, hoping it would be my ticket to a different future. Music was more than background noise to me. It felt like a safe space, a friend, a home where feelings were in the open, where the artists were able to discuss their personal struggles and chase their dreams. And my favorite childhood show, *The Fresh Prince of Bel-Air*, made California seem like a pretty attractive place to live.

But the *Lifestyles of the Rich and Famous* was far off—I had no idea what a "different" future would really look like, or how I would make it happen. At 12, I was enough of a realist to know I couldn't ditch seventh grade and go on a world tour for the rest of my life. However, through school I heard of an opportunity to travel to Europe and stay with some host families for the summer. Given how little I cared about school then, I'm not sure I could've identified the exact location of any country in Europe, but it didn't matter. I somehow knew taking that trip would be a down payment on a promise to spend my life seeing and doing more than Genesee County had to offer.

There was a slight hiccup in my plan: I had absolutely no money. My parents couldn't just fork over all the cash in an instant, and (legal) jobs for 12-year-olds were nonexistent.

So, I started my first "business." I bought bulk candy at Sam's Club and resold it at local bowling alleys. The typical Flint-area alley came standard with an ever-present haze of Marlboro smoke and psychedelic carpets with a permanent coating of stale Bud Light. What it lacked in sanitation, it made up for with a willing target market of half-drunk bowlers who took pity on a girl selling chocolate bars.

Business was booming for several months until my grandma noticed me wearing bowling shoes and sensed something wasn't right. She wasn't the type to worry about due process, so she promptly searched my room and found my stash of stolen shoes. I know what you're thinking...who does that? Somehow, I had convinced myself that bowling shoes were fashionable (I assure you that I did not look fashionable in any way, shape, or form). So as a perk, this budding businesswoman helped herself to several pairs of rentals.

Grandma drove me to Galaxy Lanes, where I sheepishly apologized to the manager and handed him the hoard of shoes. [Insert sound of a sad trombone here.] Banned from the bowling alley. First hustle over.

But Grandma had an idea. She wanted to ease the sting of crushing my first business empire, and she wanted to help my rebellious soul find God. So, she bribed me to read the Bible. Or more precisely, to copy passages down on paper to make sure I was actually reading it. I still remember being confused about God creating light *before* the sun and stars.

I stayed up late for weeks to copy enough to satisfy her quota. Between my candy enterprise and Grandma's Bible bribes, I had gathered enough to get to Europe. For the first time in what would become hundreds, I stepped onto a plane. I still remember getting off the flight in London and thinking that "customs" was where they taught you the customs of the country. So much to learn.

I spent a few weeks in England with the student group. We weren't exactly staying at the Ritz Carlton (the only variety of Ritz I knew was the cracker) and I subsisted on a healthy diet of McDonald's chicken nuggets. Prior to the trip, the extent of my knowledge of the UK was watching Princess Diana's funeral on TV, crushing on Prince William (yes, I had his poster on my wall), and knowing the words to "Wannabe" by the Spice Girls.

After England, I took a long bus ride to Denmark, where I stayed with a host family who had a daughter a couple years older than me. She begrudgingly took me to parties, we rode around Copenhagen on bikes, and she introduced me to my new favorite brand, Nutella. I remember drawing many deep lessons from this first exploration of another culture. In no particular order: 1) Eating a chocolate-like spread for breakfast was awesome, 2) Going to parties was fun, and 3) *If I want something, I can make it happen.*

✦ ✦ ✦

Something amazing happens when you have a clear vision of what you want in life and why you want it. Clarity lets you see a path forward where you never noticed one before and motivates you to take steps down that path, even if they're difficult or scary. The bowling alley and Sam's Club had always been there—I had just never thought of using them to make my own money until I'd had a compelling reason to do so. Simply put, people get to where they want to go because they know where they want to go.

In this chapter, you'll create that clear vision for yourself. The Treasure Map you made in the last chapter is a good starting point, but now you'll take it even further so you can see exactly what your future life will look like. When you create that image in your mind, you give yourself the power to achieve it.

Find Your Compass

Like many young girls, my first true musical love was boy bands. With my long blonde mop hair, I pretended I was a member of Hanson (and thanks to the relative lack of internet, some people actually believed me). When 'N Sync was signing albums at the Harmony House record store down the street, I invited the newly famous Justin Timberlake to my 13th birthday party (sadly, my dream lover did not attend). I wasn't exactly what you would call "popular" among the other kids (more of a "marching band and choir" type of kid), and I used these fantasies as an escape.

Luckily for me and everyone else I knew, I discovered my parents' record collection and moved on to worshiping the gods of rock for the next few years: Led Zeppelin, The

Beatles, Tom Petty, Pink Floyd, AC/DC, Queen, you name it. I knew every lyric, every chord change and drumbeat, every fact about each member of each band. I covered my room in posters, wore band tees exclusively, sketched out band logos on my notebooks during class, camped outside venues to buy concert tickets, (embarrassingly) registered my AOL screen name as "rockstarwannabe," hung out every weekend at the all-ages rock club Flint Local 432, scraped together enough cash to buy a used drum set and guitar, and tried to sell my soul for rock and roll at several points. Each night, I dreamed of touring the globe, hanging out with rockstars, and reveling in my ideal life. After all, my favorite movie was *Almost Famous*.

I had put no thought into any "professional" field other than music, but at the same time, I had absolutely no connections (Michigan isn't exactly a booming entertainment metropolis), so my chances of becoming the next Rick Rubin were very slim. So, I looked to those who had done it before. I spent hours in the library reading biographies of people who had achieved what I wanted, many of whom had it *way* worse than I did when they started out. If they could do it, so could I, even though there were several massive obstacles: 1) I knew exactly zero people who had done *anything* in the music business, 2) Everyone said I was being unrealistic, and 3) I lived in a place that wasn't conducive to the dream.

So, to put the gears in motion on my rock-and-roll fantasy, I did every "get-your-foot-in-the-door" job you can imagine. I handed out thousands of flyers, fetched coffee at radio stations, sold band merchandise out of vans in a million cookie-cutter towns, worked "security" at an amphitheater (which sadly meant taking bongs from Grateful Dead fans outside the gates), and skipped events like prom and homecoming to pick up never-ending mounds of trash off the floor at grimy clubs and festivals like Warped Tour...for $5 an hour.

I knew that the path to the music industry wasn't through a traditional classroom, so I found a loophole at my high school where I could graduate a year early if I worked enough hours outside school. My parents understandably didn't want me sitting around smoking pot all day (they had enough to worry about), so I enrolled in the local community college—not to attend the actual classes, but to act like I was while I sat in the library and read band autobiographies. The day I turned 18, I "dropped out" (does it count if I never went to a class?) and started working even more hours at my two minimum wage jobs: one at the local concert and NBA arena and one at the mall. A real university was never an option anyway—my greatest academic accomplishment was getting a free pepperoni pizza for Pizza Hut's "Book It" program.

This was my version of an education and the building blocks to the experiences I knew I wanted.

One magical day, I was restocking the latest Eminem CD near the entrance of the mall record store, and I noticed someone on a Blackberry (a phone that was considered fancy then) counting the albums. Could this be it? My chance? *Score!* It was indeed a representative from the largest record label in the world, checking out the local stores to see how the album was selling during release week.

I promptly dropped all responsibilities and focused on begging this poor guy to tell me who hired interns at the label. He eventually broke down and gave me a general company email address so I would leave him alone.

After emailing them incessantly until they responded with an application, I did the most underrated thing you can do on a resume. I...lied. I had been familiar with this particular creative method since age 15, when I embellished my age to write album reviews ($15 apiece!) for the local newspaper, *The Flint Journal*. I'm absolutely not advocating for adding "Harvard Doctorate" to your resume if you completed one semester of community college, but this little teenage perjury seemed completely harmless and brought me closer to the life I envisioned.

Specifically, I said I was going to college, which made me eligible to apply for an unpaid internship at Universal Music Group's Detroit office. I fabricated a letter from the local university with assistance from Microsoft Paint so I could get a "job" that paid nothing. If any authorities are reading this, I promise to pay back all the money I never made as a result of my dishonesty.

This led to a desperate lifestyle that included stealing toilet paper from the office, searching through friends' couch cushions for coins, eating more than my fair share of Chipotle burritos at catered meetings, and occasionally getting treated to lunch from any coworker nice enough to take pity on me when I "forgot" my wallet. It's hard to get an apartment without any income, so my sleeping options ranged from my car to the 13 different floors I called home. During one of my longer-term couch stays, our heat got shut off in January, so my friends and I pooled together $20 to buy a space heater and slept on the floor next to it for the rest of the frigid winter.

And then, all my efforts paid off. I was hired by the label to work in the mailroom and earn *twenty thousand dollars a year*. Are you freaking kidding me? $20k! *MTV Cribs*, here I come! Before you laugh too hard at 19-year-old me, remember that $20,000 a year sounded very good compared to $0 a year. Also, over 100 people had applied for that mailroom job, so I felt like I had won the lottery. I was on cloud nine and can still remember the moment I found out: pure elation. *I fucking made it.*

✦ ✦ ✦

What would make *you* feel this way? What do you long to become? What are you willing to work hard for and make sacrifices to achieve?

I'll be honest, most of the stuff I did in those early days would not have made it onto my Treasure Map. Would I have picked up trash in clubs and put up flyers in the freezing cold if I only had a year left to live? Absolutely not. But I did know I wanted to be in the music business, and there was no magic lamp to rub to make my wishes come true.

Those experiences were essential because they put me on the path to my long-term ambitions.

The Treasure Map exercise is a powerful way to spark urgency and articulate what matters to you, but it's missing the long-term perspective. After all, if you only have a year, a month, or a day left to live, there's no time to build something like a career, a family, or a business. So while it's true that any day could be your last, and you definitely shouldn't put off your dreams until "someday," we're not suggesting that you *literally* live as if you'll die tomorrow. If you do that, you'll never invest in building something for the future.

Those long-term projects will be the most fulfilling and impactful things you ever do—you definitely don't want to leave them out of your vision. You need both ends of the spectrum: the urgent, must-do items and the grand, multiyear ambitions. People tend to overestimate what they can do in one year and underestimate what they can do in 10 years.

So, back to the question at hand: What do you want to build for yourself? What's the compass guiding the overall direction of your life?

I fixated on a direction early in life, but many people don't. If you didn't have a passion that grabbed you in your childhood or teen years, you probably followed whatever path seemed most prudent or interesting at the time—or whatever path someone else said you should take. You may have developed a passion along the way...but maybe not. It's incredibly common for people in their thirties, forties, and beyond to still not have a clear sense of what they want to do with their lives.

If that's you, it's worth taking the time to find your compass. As we've established, time is precious, and you don't want to waste it floundering around when you could be using it to build or become something you really want. That last bit is crucial—it has to be what you genuinely want, not what someone else wants for you, no matter how much you might love and respect that person. It's your life, not theirs, and you only get one.

One place to start is your Treasure Map. Are there any themes that immediately become clear? For example, if I had made a Treasure Map at age 17, it would have included things like seeing my favorite artists perform, going to music festivals, becoming proficient at guitar and drums, traveling the world, and living in a big city like LA or New York. Obviously, the signs of my obsession with entertainment were there.

Can you see signs of your compass on your Treasure Map? Maybe there are lots of experiences related to nature, travel, family, sports, art, food, or some other common thread. If so, you should seriously consider orienting your life in that direction. If you would spend your last year on earth in nature but you currently work in a cubicle and live in a concrete jungle, something needs to change (an example that became glaringly clear to me in my own life later on).

Another way to find your compass is to pay attention to your daydreams. Research suggests 30 to 50 percent of our time is spent daydreaming.[7] While this fact seems pretty crazy considering it's half our waking hours, those daydreams can shine a light on what you might *actually* want to be doing. So, the next time you feel your mind wandering, write down what you're thinking about. Do this for a few days or weeks, and you'll probably start to see some themes emerge.

If these exercises aren't giving you any obvious clues, we highly recommend you take a deeper dive into finding your compass. There are whole books written on the subject,[8,9,10] so we won't attempt to rehash them here. The key thing to understand now is that enthusiasm needs direction—all the urgency in the world won't give you a meaningful life if you don't know what to do with it.

If you already have a compass for your life, that's wonderful. Write it down in big, bold letters at the top of your Treasure Map.

If not, don't stress. You don't have to stop everything and figure it out *today*—this isn't something you can force. It's a discovery process, so keep digging. Ask yourself why you do what you do. Pay attention to your curiosity and desire. If you stay aware, the picture will become clearer over time.

Refine Your Treasure Map

Once you identify a clear direction for your life, go back to your Treasure Map. As I said, it's a great way to start thinking about what you want, but it's not a complete vision yet. We're about to make it one.

First, add activities that are related to the long-term goals you just articulated. For example, if you want to become a film director, film school and networking with like-minded people should be listed. If you want to find "the one" and start a family, make sure you know what you are looking for long-term, intentionally find people who fit that criteria, and start putting yourself in social situations where people like that will be in attendance.

Now, take a closer look at each of the items on your Treasure Map and do a gut check: Is this really what *you* want? Does the desire come from your heart and soul...or does it come from your family, your friends, social media, societal expectations, or some other place outside you? Be careful—according to *The Top Five Regrets of the Dying*, the number one deathbed regret is, "I wish I'd had the courage to live a life true to myself, not the life others expected of me."[11] This is your life. Don't let it get hijacked by other people.

Next we have a slightly more complex question: How do these experiences contribute to your experiential wealth? I mean, what makes an experience enriching anyway? To aid in answering this, we've identified five key factors. Look at each item on your Treasure Map and ask yourself these five questions:

1. **Does it support your well-being?** Using your body, fueling it right, relieving stress—if you want to live life to the fullest, you've got to take care of yourself, which can be a valuable experience in itself.

2. **Does it nurture important relationships?** Spending quality time with loved ones, meeting new people, being part of a team—these experiences build the strong social ties we human beings need to thrive.

3. **Does it make you grow?** Exploration, discovery, challenge, learning, practice—it might be hard sometimes, but that's part of what makes it so valuable.

4. **Does it bring you joy?** Play, entertainment, thrills, peace, wonder, silliness, laughter—anything that brings more of this stuff to your life is a keeper.

5. **Does it serve others?** Giving your time, energy, and money to help those who need it—that's the legacy you'll leave behind when all is said and done.

Each item on your list should get at least one yes. If it doesn't, cross it off—it's not adding enough value to your life to be a high priority.

Ideally, across your Treasure Map, you would have at least one yes for each of these five questions. Each one speaks to an essential part of a fulfilling, meaningful life. So, while you don't need to have perfect balance across the five, it's wise not to neglect any one of them completely.

Don't worry about solving that just yet. Later, we'll explore why these themes are important and show you how to incorporate each one into your life.

Tell Your Own Fortune

Back at work, my daydreams had turned into reality. In between licking stamps and mailing boxes, my tasks included playing "security" for Sting at a bookstore filled with drooling older women, taking Rihanna to TGI Fridays, finding drugs for family-friendly singer songwriters [names redacted], watching pop punk bands sort through groupies [names also redacted], building the label's first Myspace page, making a birthday cake for LL Cool J, convincing Detroit strip clubs to play Nine Inch Nails' new single, watching Steel Panther air hump my CEO's head in the conference room, and being on the receiving end of an office eviction notice after a particularly loud visit from Kanye West. I'm pretty sure my career peaked when I was asked to judge an air guitar competition on VH1.

Then, when I was 21, I got called into my boss' office and heard the devastating words so many people are familiar with: "We're going to have to lay you off. Our branch is shutting down." Just when I had reached a point where I could survive, I was out of a job and completely devastated. Back to square one. I thought my life and dreams were over.

It was the best thing that had ever happened to me. I just didn't know it yet.

While living off paltry unemployment checks for six months, I learned to do basic coding and web design. I finally ended up getting a decent job offer in a different, more "stable" industry, but, even though I was eating "sleep" for dinner several nights a week, accepting the position didn't feel right. When I visualized my future after trading in my life in music for something "easier" and "safer," it looked like a dream killer. I saw myself trudging into an office of people I couldn't relate to, in pantsuits instead of leather jackets, to live inside Microsoft Excel selling products I didn't believe in, day in and day out. I saw myself reluctantly settling for what I had sworn to escape, my dreams getting buried for the status quo. That was *not* what I wanted my life to look like. So, I took a big risk and turned down the job, much to the horror of everyone around me.

Then, the week my unemployment ran out, I got a very timely phone call from Warner Music Group in Burbank, California, where I had applied for a job where my new design skills would be an asset. "We can't offer you more than $27,000 a year," they said, "but we promise lots of free food, drinks, concerts, and epic experiences." So, like many lost souls before me, I made the biggest decision of my life and struck out for Hollywood. I spent my last $100 on a one-way, two-stop, middle-seat, Spirit Airlines ticket—and left everything I knew behind for the far away land of opportunity I had dreamed of as a child.

As little as this salary provided in Los Angeles, my gut had made the right decision. I had to have four roommates (that I met on Craigslist) to make rent in a dilapidated, moldy house in the San Fernando Valley, but my childhood dreams had come true. I got to work with my idols up close and personal in the creative and entertainment capital of the world—with the perk of nearly 300 days of sunshine a year. No more scraping ice off my windshield with used CD cases! Over the next five years, I attended thousands of shows and festivals around the country. I hung out nightly at legendary venues I had read about as a kid, like the Troubadour, the Whisky a Go Go, and the Hollywood Bowl. I met larger-than-life figures such as Mick Jagger, Neil Young, U2, and The Who. I got a front row seat to the rise of artists like Taylor Swift, Drake, Jack Johnson, Justin Bieber, The Killers, Lady Gaga, Amy Winehouse, and The Weeknd.

As an added bonus to following my passion, for the first time in my life, I felt surrounded by people who inspired me, energized me, and made me feel part of a community. My friends were lovable music geeks who would sit at a dive bar or around a campfire with me and enthusiastically discuss the intricacies of the production on OK Computer, make wristbands out of ribbons to sneak into the Coachella VIP, or happily wait outside for a full day to get into a secret Foo Fighters show at a 100-person capacity club. I worked as an assistant for powerful executives who introduced me to a big city life on a company credit card. I got to tag along to fancy restaurants, movie premieres, and parties in the Hollywood Hills. I could have never dreamed of this had I stayed in my comfort zone.

I was still broke.

But anything seemed possible now.

✦ ✦ ✦

I could have played it safe and taken the more corporate job back home, like everyone said I should. I almost did. It was only that terrifying visualization of a future far down the wrong path that stopped me from settling and gave me the courage to make a "risky" move in the direction I truly wanted to go.

Visualization won't make things magically happen, but it's still a powerful tool. It gives you clarity in the face of hard choices. It motivates you to do things that are hard but necessary to achieve your goals. It even helps you shed limiting beliefs about who you are and what you're capable of. You may not think of yourself as someone who can scale the face of a mountain, publish a book, or plant a million trees, but the more you visualize yourself doing it, the more plausible it feels.

In these ways, visualization can help you define and achieve your vision of an ideal life. And luckily, anyone can do it, anywhere, at any time. Visualization techniques are all about generating a detailed mental picture. This picture can motivate you, clarify your decisions, relieve anxiety, and increase focus. In some ways, our brains can't distinguish between reality and imagination; brain scans of people doing an activity look the same as those of people visualizing the same activity.[12]

Because visualization can have a real impact on how you think and feel, it's so important to visualize the future you want—especially if it feels distant or hard to reach. When you imagine it in great detail, you bring it closer in a very real way.

That said, fantasies of your desires aren't much use unless they lead to action. Visualizing what you want gives you focus and clarity, but it also gives your brain a dopamine hit. That moment of pleasure can make you complacent, as if the fantasy itself is enough. Obviously, it's not.

So, don't just imagine the end goal—visualize the process to get there as well, including all the obstacles and failures you might experience along the way. Imagine what will happen if you don't take action toward your dream, as I did when I thought about taking that boring job after getting laid off. That "negative" visualization is just as important as imagining success. In fact, it's been shown that thinking about failure or inaction makes people twice as likely to achieve their goals.[13]

We'll put this into practice at the end of this chapter where we'll walk you through an exercise to visualize the big dreams you've laid out on your Treasure Map.

Let Your Vision Evolve

As time went on, I started becoming aware that my priorities would change as I got older. I had originally visualized staying in the music industry forever, but after five years of cubicles and daily back-to-back meetings followed by sex, drugs, and rock-and-roll fueled nights at Hollywood clubs, I knew I couldn't keep it up for the rest of my life. I realized that how I was then wasn't always how I would be. I felt a deep yearning to see the world and experience cultures and businesses outside of entertainment, and I started brainstorming ways to make enough money to replace my meager salary.

One day at my office, I came across a random viral YouTube video. It was of a 29-year-old woman named Sloane who was able to hear for the very first time thanks to a special kind of hearing aid. It was an irresistibly joyful and moving scene, and people couldn't get enough—it even snowballed to the point that she ended up on *Ellen*.

Sloane's experience was powerful. It's obvious to the millions who saw the video that it was life-changing for her... but its power didn't stop there.

Because when I saw that video, it got me thinking about how different my life would have been without sound. How my life path had changed because of my compass—music. And it gave me an idea.

I sent the video to Joe, who was helping build schools in Guatemala at the time. He was the only person I knew who was involved in charity work. Before I met him, I had thought philanthropy was a walled garden filled with $10,000 tables and black tuxes, something reserved for the super elite—but neither of us were that. So when Joe and I met, we instantly felt like family, maybe in part because we both came from humble beginnings. We wanted more than our backgrounds had predicted for us, and we felt a persistent tug to help others who were living less-than-easy lives.

Joe watched the video and listened to my idea: to start a brand that would sell headphones and speakers and use the proceeds to give hearing aids to people in need, just like in the video. It would be the world's first social good electronics company. He jumped on board instantly, and I put in my two weeks' notice and cashed out my life savings—my 401k from Universal Music Group had accumulated a whopping $5,000. (It turns out working with superstars doesn't mean you have the bank account of one.)

We high-fived and jumped on a plane to China, without a business plan or any idea on how the electronics industry worked, to source products for our new social enterprise, LSTN (pronounced "listen"). We filled my apartment's kitchen with as much inventory as we could buy, handmade our own headphone packaging with boxes from the local Michael's craft store, cobbled together a website, worked our asses off, and prayed. Hard.

And, just four years later, we sold to Apple for $3 billion dollars!

Just kidding—we are not Dr. Dre. This is not a rags-to-riches story about making billions from selling headphones.

But it *is* a different kind of rags-to-riches story.

Because almost exactly a year after first seeing that video of Sloane and visualizing doing the same thing, Joe and I found ourselves in a gymnasium in Piura, Peru, with a young girl named Maria.

Like the hundreds of others there that day who had traveled from all over Peru, often great distances under difficult circumstances, she came with the hope of hearing for the first time. This being our very first day as volunteers with Starkey Hearing Foundation—our new company's philanthropic partner—we were especially excited that our station was the last step, where hearing aids would be fitted and tested. She sat down in the hard plastic chair in front of us, nervous and full of anxiety and hope. I was in charge of fitting her hearing aids and gently pushed one into each of Maria's ears.

What happened next was one of those moments in life that bursts at the seams and can never be fully captured on a two-dimensional page.

Maria's eyes went wide, and then a look of pure wonder flashed across her face. Her astonished joy delivered the moment of truth: she could hear.

Tears flowed from her parents as they collapsed on the floor in relief. Overpowered, we cried, too.

What started off as a farfetched dream had turned into the closest thing to a miracle we had ever seen.

This was all possible because I had allowed my dreams to evolve and grow over time.

Like mine, your vision is not set in stone. It will change as you get older, discover new things, and meet new people—and that's okay. You may find that after years or even decades pursuing the same thing, you've gotten everything out of it that you can, or it turned out to be different from what you expected, or it just doesn't excite you the way it once did.

Stay attuned to those feelings. As risky as it may feel to change course, the greater risk is staying in a career, business, or relationship even when it no longer feels right. Sadly, people do this *all the time*. They get trapped by golden handcuffs, trading years of misery for shiny benefits they may or may not live to enjoy. Or they look back at all the time and effort they've invested in their path and can't bear to see it go to "waste." Or they feel overwhelmed by the challenge of starting something new.

People get scared because it's easier to wrap their heads around what they have to lose than what they have to gain. What they don't think about is the opportunity cost—the years of potential joy, fulfillment, and growth they'll lose if they continue on their current path. As I've learned firsthand, even the worst day doing something you love is better than the best day doing something you hate.

So, don't be afraid to let your vision evolve. Just because you change course doesn't mean all your previous efforts were for nothing. They made you who you are and brought you to this point. Those experiences will always be part of your story, and they'll continue to influence you for the rest of your life. You'll have the comfort of knowing you did those things, and even though you grew out of them, you'll never regret doing them in the first place.

You Control Your Crystal Ball

Spoiler alert: Launching and growing our beloved social enterprise was a wild and rough road, littered with crushing disappointments as well as major victories. But thanks to being clear on what we wanted to accomplish, we were able to ride out the roller coaster.

As massive companies like Amazon, Spotify, and Facebook started to see value in our philanthropic mission, our public profile skyrocketed. We starred in commercials by Google and Delta Air Lines. We were interviewed by the *Today Show*, *Good Morning America*, and the *New York Times*. We received fan letters from US presidents and Kim Kardashian. We hosted our own segments on QVC. People even tattooed graphics of our products on their bodies (true story, questionable idea). It seemed like my whole life I'd been chasing my dreams, and now my dreams were chasing me.

I was shocked when I made it on both the *Forbes* and *Inc Magazine* 30 Under 30 lists—there was no way I belonged there...not unless they meant 30 people with less than $30. People I knew from all facets of my life reached out and said, "Wow, it looks like you're killing it!" and of course, "Hey, I know we haven't talked since high school...but can I borrow some money?" Nope—I still had to check my balance before filling my car with gas. As many startup founders know too well, the difference between what we were worth "on paper" and what we actually had was astronomical—off by tens of millions of dollars. We were surviving and happy, but giving away far more money to our charity partner than we paid ourselves. We never became the biggest brand in the space, and we never raised a ton of capital or sold out to a global conglomerate.

But that was never the vision, as we were reminded on a trip to Uganda. This particular day, we were at Sister Rosemary's incredibly transformative school for girls in war-torn Gulu, on our ninth straight day of 6 a.m. to 11 p.m. mission work.

Joe and I sat on dusty plastic chairs in the scorching heat, eating rice with Bill Austin, the founder of Starkey Technologies and a self-made multi-billionaire. I was 28; he was 73 and had been absolutely running laps around me all day. It had been a particularly rough day. Even though the patients were mostly under eight years old, they had already been through horrific times in Joseph Kony's Lord's Resistance Army. They had lost limbs and seen family members get murdered. Their precious childhoods had become irrecoverable. It was a very dark scene.

Until then, I had seen the likes of this on television, but I hadn't been remotely prepared for this in real life. It was crushing my soul and I was mentally and physically exhausted. In a weak moment, I asked Bill why, if he could do literally *anything* he wanted, he chose to spend all his time traveling to remote locations to help others. Why not just take a break, get massages, and sip daiquiris under a thatched roof on an aqua beach in Bora Bora for a few months?

He replied with something that will stick with me for the rest of my life: "*You can always make more money, but you can never make more time.*" He explained that he was in a race against time to change as many lives as he could—and as a bonus had gotten to see corners of the Earth that most people never will. That was his compass. And by filling the time he had left with this purpose, he was fulfilling his ideal self.

It reinforced our own motives for following our dreams. We responded and said while we may never amass great monetary wealth like he had, we considered ourselves to be *experiential* billionaires. He laughed at our attempted joke and told us we had some catching up to do. Our exhaustion transformed into inspiration—and we got to work with Bill and Starkey Hearing Foundation all around the world for another six years, helping to give the gift of hearing to over 50,000 individuals. It would be an understatement to say that watching kids' eyes light up as they heard music, rain, or someone saying "I love you" for the first time changed my life and the way I viewed the world, forever.

✦ ✦ ✦

EXERCISE

Visualize Your Future

1. Look at your Treasure Map again. Based on this chapter, do you see any glaring gaps? Is there anything you would add or change? If you haven't yet, write down a word or two at the top that describes your compass. Common examples are "family," "travel," "outdoor adventures," "find peace," and "new skills." Remember your compass when you feel like you're getting off track.

2. Focus on the biggest, most ambitious dream on your Treasure Map. Close your eyes and visualize it in as

much detail as possible. For example, let's say you want to start your own business. Is it a restaurant? A boutique clothing store? A design agency? Imagine working on it. What would be the best location? Can you visualize yourself waking up to a day in that life? What does your schedule look like? What do you see, hear, feel, smell, and taste? What emotions do you experience?

3. Then, visualize what will happen if you *don't* take steps toward building that life. You'll be stuck where you are now—wishing for this dream—only it will be worse, because you'll know what it could have felt like. Imagine the worst-case scenario later in life as you continue choosing to not follow your dreams. Play through a day in that life in just as much detail as the day in your dream life.

4. Write down what you visualized. When you lose focus on this dream, go back to what you wrote and try to visualize it again.

5. (Optional) If you have no idea what the path to your goals might look like, learn from others. Is it your dream to climb Kilimanjaro, but you don't know anyone who has done this? Do you have a burning desire to start a nonprofit organization in your community, but you've never met anyone who works

in charity? It's time to consult your new mentors, found on YouTube and in books. Learn from those who have done it before, take notes on how they did what you want to do, and even reach out to them. You might be surprised at how willing people are to help you achieve your dreams.

Note: Go to ExperientialBillionaire.com *to download or print an extended version of this exercise in addition to free experience guides.*

PART II

Uncover The Path

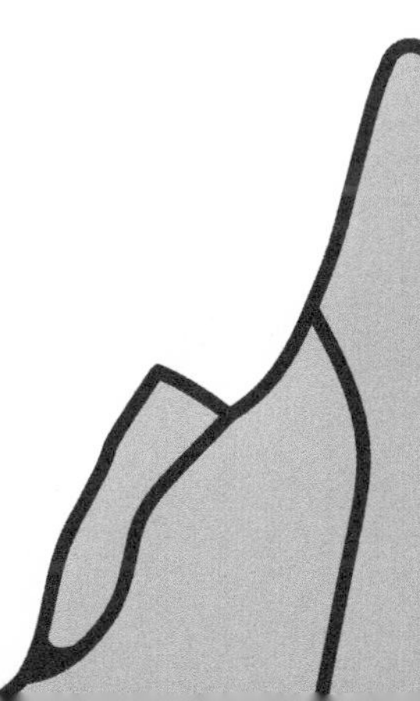

Chapter Three

TAKE RADICAL RESPONSIBILITY

“Most powerful is he who has himself in his own power.”

—Seneca

Joe:

"I'm sorry. You've been expelled from school."

It was 9:15 in the morning a few weeks into September, and all the other kids were in the middle of their first period class, just like they had been for the last two weeks. I, however, had only just showed up that day to register for what was supposed to be my junior year of high school. Two. Weeks. Late.

My guidance counselor's words were clear: That was no longer an option. For a few long moments, she looked at me with what seemed more like empathy—or maybe just plain sadness—than consternation before abruptly standing and sending me back home.

It was still a few years before my dad's heart transplant. I was blissfully unaware of the potential consequences of my actions, and my parents were blissfully unaware of my transgressions. By then, I had built up a solid array of excuses to deflect responsibility for my abundant screwups...which had been extremely useful, as I was in the midst of a life-derailing drug addiction.

My foray into drugs started out small and seemingly harmless. Unfortunately, it only took me a couple of years to go from sneaking behind the school to smoke some joints with my friends to stealing my parent's car, driving to a crack house at 3 a.m., and selling my mom's wedding ring for $50 worth of blow to a guy named One-Armed Larry. That's one experience I'd like to forget. But this story isn't about drugs. It's about excuses—something I had become extremely good at.

I thought excuses enabled me to get away with things. They certainly had up to that point. In reality, they only bought me a massive life debt that would have to be repaid one day—and that day had finally come. As I walked home, I was unable to think of a single excuse to escape the fact that I had just been expelled from school.

At this point, you might be wondering, *Where were your parents? How did it get this far before they noticed anything?* They were trying, they really were. But, like a lot of parents in my neighborhood, they worked all day and trusted me home alone under the not-so-watchful supervision of my two older brothers. This was pretty normal back then, at least in my neck of the woods. And it usually worked out. Usually.

I'll never forget the look of shattered hope and utter disappointment on their faces when I broke the news. My mom burst into tears. My dad just went gravely quiet. They both worked so hard to provide for their children, and my older brothers had both graduated and become independent adults. School hadn't been an issue for me for *most* of my life; I had always brought home good grades. When that changed during my sophomore year, I hid it from them with report card forgeries and other lies, which I justified in my own mind with—you guessed it—excuses.

That was the moment I understood a fundamental truth, one that would guide me through many of life's most difficult challenges: Excuses don't matter. They don't fix anything. They deflect and distract us from what we really want and need. They stop us from taking responsibility for our lives. Instead of solving our problems, excuses just kick the can down the road.

I had thought that road would lead to the future my friends and I dreamed about—the rich life we saw on TV: Luxury cars. Lavish vacations. Expensive dinners. Suddenly, I realized where it would actually take me: Jail. Unemployment. Rehab. Health issues. Financial instability.

I did not want to go there. As cool as I thought it had been to be a rebel, I hadn't stopped to think I might be throwing my life away. So, I asked myself a really hard question, maybe the hardest question I had ever asked: What would happen if I stopped making excuses and actually took responsibility for my one and only life? Could I recover from my mistakes and salvage my future?

Maybe, and that was good enough for me to give it my best shot.

First, I had to get help to stop using drugs. Thankfully, I got it from friends, family, and professionals. My mom, in particular, who I forced to endure many tortured and sleepless nights, was unwavering in her support and unconditional love. It was a long and bumpy road, but it was enough to get me headed back in the right direction and ready to tackle an even bigger obstacle: graduating from high school.

Although I had been expelled, I could still enroll in continuation school. In our area, that was usually a stepping stone to one of two things: getting your GED or dropping out of school. But in theory, if I could squeeze my sophomore and junior year coursework into one year, I could get back into the mainstream high school for my senior year and graduate on time with my class. Hard? Yes. Possible? Maybe.

I threw myself into the challenge with no holds barred. I read entire textbooks at warp speed. I took tests every day for most of the year. I didn't miss a single day of school. Instead of making excuses, I made plans and set goals.

To everyone's disbelief (including mine), it worked. I returned to my regular high school for my senior year. I graduated, proving to my friends, my community, my parents, and, most importantly, myself that I could overcome difficult situations. I could accomplish hard things when I stopped making excuses. I wasn't going to hide behind excuses and watch my life slip away. It might not sound like a big deal that I "only" graduated high school, but to me it felt like being valedictorian at Yale.

The moral here is simple: You are in control of your life, much more than you realize or at times want to admit. Yes, there's plenty of stuff in the world that's out of your hands. But you always have a choice about what you do.

Most of the time, our own internal voices get in the way. We tell ourselves stories about what we can't do and lay the blame on other people, the economy, the universe—anywhere but at our own feet. That's easier than admitting that we can do something, but we've *chosen* not to.

Correction: It's easier in the moment, but in the long run, it only compounds your problems and limits your possibilities.

In my sophomore year of high school, I chose not to study or go to class, and I blamed those choices on everyone and everything but me. That didn't protect me from the consequences, and your excuses won't protect you either. When you recognize that, you can stop waiting and complaining and start taking radical responsibility for your one precious life. If you don't, no one else will.

So, what are your excuses? Here are a few from the excuses hall of fame: *I don't have the money. I don't have the time. I'm afraid of failing. I just haven't gotten around to it.*

Sound familiar? They should. Those were the top answers from our 20,000+ global *Life Experiences Survey* respondents when we asked why they hadn't done the things they wanted to do. We use these things to justify putting things off that we really want out of life. They are all just variations of the same disease: excuses.

Let's start off with the elephants in the room: money and time. It's time to sweep these excuses away and clear your path, because they're just holding you back from the life you really want to live. The stories in this chapter are proof of that, and the exercises at the end will show you how to go from making excuses to making actual plans for your future. Make sure you do them. Inspiration is cool but action will make the difference between dreaming about a life rich in experiences and living it.

Overcoming the "Money Problem"

At age 27, I filed for personal bankruptcy.

I know, you must be shocked that my post-high school life wasn't a fairy tale where everything magically worked out. I had learned my lesson about excuses, and my dad's health scare had armed me with the urgency to make the most of my life. But I still made mistakes, and that year, a few too many of them combined to spark financial disaster.

For work, I drove around doing quality control inspections of giant bales of recyclable materials bound for overseas. It was exactly as glamorous as it sounds. I had decent pay and flexible hours, but I was a contractor, which meant I had to pay my own taxes. I neglected to do this for three years before I realized that was a bad long-term strategy and decided to clean it up.

Not wanting to break my streak of good decisions, I hired a guy named Tattoo Tony to do my taxes (yes, he had a lot of tattoos). I signed off on all the returns, sent them to the IRS, and promptly forgot all about it. Looking back, I'm thinking the IRS probably flags people filing back taxes as good candidates for an audit. Or people who use Tattoo Tony. Hindsight, as they say, is 20/20.

It was about a year after filing all those tax forms that I received an audit notice. I wasn't thrilled with the hassle, but I figured I was fine. After all, Tattoo Tony had done my taxes. What could go wrong? The red flags had been due to some clerical mistakes Tattoo Tony had made in the filing, but once the IRS was in the door, they wanted to go back further than the past three years. I couldn't come up with the documentation they wanted. For the IRS, no documentation means it didn't happen, which meant I had a huge tax bill and penalties, too.

I might have been able to pay that bill, but around the same time, I went on a 24-hour snowboarding trip to the local mountains. That turned out to be just enough time to lose control on some black ice and total my car...two days after I had accidentally let my car insurance lapse. That was the final Jenga block on top of my teetering finances, and everything came crashing down.

I suddenly found myself considering a desperate course of action: bankruptcy. Once filed, it would take about 10 years to fully recover my financial status and creditworthiness. *Ten years* of hustling and scrimping to erase debts and rebuild my credit score. I visited a bankruptcy attorney, who calmly explained that the fee for filing bankruptcy was $2,500. It was like getting kicked when I was already down, but it did have one benefit. It gave me a great line for my stand-up comedy routine: "So now I've gotta go around telling people I'd like to be bankrupt, but I just can't afford it."

EXPERIENCES CAN BE FREE

I was dead broke. It was the perfect excuse to not do things... but I had already learned all the good making excuses would do for me.

Instead, I focused on what was in my power. I started hiking the Santa Monica mountains at sunrise every single morning. Between shifts at work, I came home and skateboarded through the winding, tree-covered streets of the Hollywood Hills with my 180-pound Rottweiler rescue, Kodi-bear, who thought he was a Golden Retriever. I started journaling before bed every night and became seriously interested in longer-form writing.

I didn't allow my lack of money to become a reason for stagnation. I didn't put my life on hold or wait until I somehow had enough money to do that one big thing. I did what I could do at the time with the little (or nothing) I had to spare.

To this day, those are some of the most valuable experiences I've ever had. The sunrise hikes not only lifted my spirits to start each and every day (which was necessary to face the uphill battle of rebuilding my life) but also helped me get into great physical shape. Skateboarding required most of my concentration and was extremely therapeutic as a way to calm my mind—besides being outdoors in a beautiful environment with my dog, whose companionship alone was therapeutic. Journaling was cathartic and helped me move through things. So, while those activities didn't directly increase my net worth at the time, they helped me grow stronger mentally and physically, which I knew would be helpful in facing whatever may lay ahead. And I seriously enjoyed (and still do) all of those activities, so forming those healthy habits was time well spent.

An empty wallet is not a fun feeling, we know. There's a special kind of stress that comes with not being able to pay the bills. Money definitely contributes to your well-being. It allows you to eat well, educate your kids, put gas in your car, and pay medical bills—in other words, address a lot of critical problems in life.

That said, money is a *means*, not a *meaning*. Wealth influences a small variance in levels of happiness, and the pursuit of wealth itself doesn't create happiness. Most importantly, you do not have to be wealthy to have an experience-rich life. Some of my most memorable and valuable experiences happened when I was flat broke.

This may sound like I'm just placating you. Don't get me wrong—if someone said to me, "You don't need to go on a safari—just go to the local zoo instead!" I'd probably want to punch them in the face. I certainly know that big, expensive experiences can be some of the most magical, and you should absolutely seek ways to plan and achieve them. For example, gorilla trekking in Rwanda wasn't cheap—it took us a long time to plan and save for it—but it was an extraordinary experience.

However, that doesn't mean your high-ticket bucket list is the right place to start. You could wind up sitting on your couch wasting your life while you wait endlessly for that magical experience to become possible. Don't fall into that trap. The way to move forward is by going after what's within your reach. While you're busy exploring all the free and low-cost experiences that are right in front of you, you can start planning the expensive ones down the road. Just don't wait for only the big ones, because if you do, you just might miss out on all the easy, everyday experiences that add up to so much value. As Oscar Wilde once said, "Anyone who lives within their means suffers from a lack of imagination."

For example, the entrance fee to any US national park? $35. Bourbon trail in Kentucky? $20. Ferry to Martha's Vineyard in Massachusetts? $17. Getty Center in California? $15. Hoover Dam in Nevada? $10. Hundreds of incredible museums around the world? Just pay to park. Step-by-step instructions on how to make an incredible Indian dinner for your family? Free on YouTube. Hikes just about anywhere? Free. If you get creative and think locally, you'll find plenty of valuable experiences you can have on the cheap.

EXPERIENCES CAN MAKE MONEY

If money is one of your top excuses, good news. There has never been a better time to start your own side hustle or small business...and that can be one of the most valuable experiences of all.

If you have or can learn a valuable skill or asset, there's money out there for you. These days, the platforms to help you reach it are more prolific than ever. You can rent out your extra bedroom, your car, your tools and equipment, even your parking space. You can create an online course, teach individual lessons, or sell your skills as a freelancer. You can start an online shop and sell your own products or resell other people's products.

The best part is, you can find things you already love doing and get paid for those things too. That way you can make money while sharing the experience you love with others—all while enjoying more of it.

That's what I did after I went bankrupt. I kept doing the quality control work, and I picked up extra jobs at restaurants and bars, but it wasn't enough. So, I asked myself what else I could do that people might pay me for.

Well, no one was asking for my financial advice (surprise!), but everyone wanted my fitness tips. I had been small and skinny through most of my youth, but after high school, a neighbor gave me his old gym equipment, and I put on 20 pounds of muscle. I've enjoyed working out ever since, and that home gym has moved with me to every place I've ever lived. Plus, all the hiking and skateboarding combined with eating on a very tight budget (canned tuna and baked potato again anyone?) had me looking extra lean and fit.

So, at the absolute rock bottom of bankruptcy, I scraped together a few hundred dollars to take certification courses, paint the inside of my garage, and get rubber mats for the floor and mirrors for the walls. Then, I spread the word that I would train people for slightly less than they would pay at the gym. Within about six months, I found myself doubling my annual income in just a few hours a day that had been my "free time."

I was on the road to financial recovery and buying my time back, all while doing something I loved.

The value didn't stop there. Yes, I was healthy, happy, and making money. But over the next couple years, as I built up my personal training business, I learned more about business in general, which would prove useful later. Many of my clients turned into lifelong friends, and both my personal and professional networks grew, opening up more social and career opportunities.

MONEY ISN'T THE POINT

Money itself isn't the end all be-all. Building experiential wealth isn't about throwing money at experiences and expecting them to make your life more meaningful. It's about changing your mindset and priorities so you learn to seek valuable experiences in every moment of every day. Once you reorient yourself around experiences, you'll start to see a lot more opportunities that don't require a huge cash investment.

When you see life through the lens of experiential wealth instead of material wealth, you're also training yourself to see what truly matters about other people. Instead of thinking of your coworker John as the guy who owns a Rolex and drives a Lexus, you think of John as a scuba diver and amazing sushi chef who can speak three languages and once got arrested in Tijuana for something involving a horse and border patrol. You like that John. We all like that John. Rolex and Lexus John seems pretty boring in comparison.

The point is that you can have a Rolex and a Lexus, but those things don't *define* who you are. Your experiences define who you are.

Money isn't the enemy either though. We said in the beginning that this isn't about having to choose between making money or having valuable life experiences. We all know having more money can make having more experiences possible. But it is important to realize that focusing *only* on making money is a bad strategy that will leave you feeling very empty.

Yet, this truth remains hard for people to grasp. Americans work, earn, and act as if becoming richer will automatically raise our happiness, with no limits. It's like a glitch in our psychological matrix. Money is not the end in itself. Remember that, or you might just spend all your time chasing paper and forget to live. So, stop using money as an excuse, start having the experiences you can afford now, and start saving for the bigger ones you really want.

Arrest Time Thieves

That brings us to the biggest excuse of all: "I just don't have time."

Imagine you wake up every morning to $1,440 in your bank account. Each day, you get to choose how to spend it—but there's a catch. If you don't spend it, it doesn't carry over to the next day. Someone or something else takes it. It is literally stolen from you. Lost forever. The next day you get another $1,440, and so on and so on, but all the days end with $0 and start over with $1,440.

If that were true, you would be damn sure to spend each one of those $1,440, right? You'd get creative. You'd look for things to invest in so your wealth would build up instead of just disappearing.

That's how time works. You get 1,440 minutes every single day, just like everyone else. Time is the great equalizer: we're all working with the same daily budget. But if you don't intentionally choose how to spend yours, someone or something else will choose for you. If you let today go to waste, it's gone for good. If you spend two weeks doing something you don't really want to do, those two weeks are stolen from your life forever. And guess what? Time is nonrefundable.

Time is truly our most valuable natural resource...but we don't treat it that way. In fact, people tend to be pretty oblivious about where their time goes and why. That's how they end up "busy" from dawn to dusk and yet somehow not doing anything they actually want to do. When we (mistakenly) act as if there will always be more time, we never get around to achieving our dreams and goals.

"Time" is a paradox. Something that parents of young children say all the time is that "the years are short, but the days are long." And that's how life actually is.

If you do the exercises in this chapter, we promise you'll see that you *do* have time to go after the experiences you want. But if you look at your Memento Mori chart, we can also promise you that you'll see the time you have is shorter than you think.

Think of it like an hourglass. The grains of sand are the days of your life, and before they fall, each one possesses enormous potential experiential wealth. But once it slips through the hourglass and falls to the bottom, there's no going back. Once it's spent, it's spent.

So, make sure you are spending it the way *you* want to. Your free time can go toward activities that reflect your real priorities—things you've intentionally chosen and genuinely want to do—or it can get stolen and squandered. Let's examine the usual suspects that most often steal away our time: technology, people, and work.

TECHNOLOGY

Unless you live in a cave, it should come as no surprise that technology, while a major benefit in so many ways, is also a massive time thief. We're connected to it 24/7, and the problem is that it's painstakingly designed to capture and hold our attention, *whether we want it to or not.* The average worker is interrupted every 11 minutes. We switch tasks 300-plus times a day and spend one-third of the day recovering from distractions.[14] In the age of distraction, focus is a superpower.

There's email, messages, social media, games, news, television, and more just waiting to suck you in. It's easy to minimize the cost of a few minutes here and there, but look at your screen time log and you'll see how they add up. Eighty-six percent of people check their phones within an hour of waking up. Even worse, screens screw with your perception of time, making it feel like life is flying by faster.[15] We definitely don't need that.

Realistically, you can't quit technology altogether—that ship has sailed. Technology has become the cafeteria where our information comes from. But that doesn't mean we've ceded control of what our information *diet* consists of. We can still control what we consume and how much time we spend consuming it.

To do that, we need to be aware of the difference between intentional technology use and letting yourself get caught in the vortex. Some of the conversations you have and the content you consume adds massive value to your life—sharing photos with your family, chatting with a potential client, researching something important to you, even laughing your ass off at some silly TikTok video. But if you're not careful, those devices turn into turbo-powered time wasters and sometimes even hurt you.

These are all habits that can be changed. I'll use TV as an example, but it's the same for scrolling or gaming or anything else tech related. Growing up, I watched a *lot* of TV. When I moved to the beach, I replaced most of my TV time with new activities (skateboarding, biking, attempting to surf). Those became my dominant lifelong habits, and now, even when I'm not doing those activities, I'm looking for other new or active things to do, rather than plopping down and turning on the TV. I still watch a show occasionally and love a family movie night, but TV isn't an unplanned activity used to fill up my time. I can't even begin to imagine how much that one habit change has allowed me to actually participate in life instead of just spectating.

So, take a hard look at what you've been consuming and the value it generates for you. For example:

- Messages and posts that help you stay connected to your friends and family? Great. Shiny influencer-style posts that make you feel inadequate and envious? Not so great.

- Work emails that help you get stuff done? Excellent. Back-channel Slack drama that distracts you from what matters? Boo.

- Thoughtful, unbiased content that educates you on the things you care about? Absolutely. Content that makes you feel outraged, scared, or frustrated about things outside your control? Absolutely not.

- TV, movies, and games that help you relax, have fun, and connect with other people? Yes, please. Scrolling through options aimlessly for hours only to be left feeling like a couch zombie? No, thank you.

One way to figure out exactly what's worth keeping and what's got to go is to take a tech break.[16] Eliminate every device-based activity in your life that's not absolutely necessary. In other words, turn off the TV, leave the computer at work, and send your phone back to 2004—essential calls and texts only. Hide or delete all the other apps.

All those hours you used to spend on social media, TV, video games, and more are now available for something else.

How about a tennis lesson? An adventure with your dog? Make dumplings? A game of Monopoly with your family? Now is your chance to do something you've been wanting to do but just never found the time to do.

Do this for a week, and the activities you've been missing out on as well as what you actually *miss* about your tech will be clear. Are you dying to get back into your favorite video game? By all means, plug in that PlayStation. But maybe you'd rather go for a swim every day than spend half an hour on Instagram, so that app stays deleted.

In the end, the point is to take control of your devices. Unfollow, unsubscribe, filter, block, delete. Use notification settings and schedules to minimize distractions and eliminate the triggers for compulsive tech use. Leverage all the tools at your disposal to curate what ends up in front of your eyes. That's how you protect your time from technology. Remember: if you aren't paying for it, your time is the product. Don't give it away or let it get stolen.

PEOPLE

Anything that eats up your time without giving you value in return is a time thief—even people. Every relationship requires us to invest effort and time, and that's fine and to be expected. However, some relationships provide great returns on those investments...and some don't.

Toxic people are a good example. You know, the ones who are always taking, never giving. It could be a friend, family member, coworker, or even a romantic partner. They demand your time, energy, and attention (maybe even your money and love) and just leave you feeling drained.

Surround yourself with people who make excuses and stay stuck, and you'll find yourself on that same excuse train. It sounds ruthless to say you should abandon your high school dropout friends that aren't making an effort to change, but life doesn't care. You can still have compassion for those people, but if they drain your energy or drag you down, it's important to minimize the time you spend with them.

Just like toxic assets in a wealth portfolio, these bad investments need to go. They don't pay off. These are more like money pits—they just keep costing more and more and more, and they never give anything in return. It's never advisable to throw good money after bad, so stop giving your valuable time to people who repeatedly waste it.

I'm not saying you must cut them out immediately and permanently. Sometimes you can, but it's not always that easy. What I *am* saying is to think carefully about that relationship. Put up clear, reasonable boundaries. Don't give an inch if you know they're going to take a mile. Safeguard as much of your time from them as you can, because you know they're going to steal it if they get the chance.

The Pareto principle states that for many outcomes, roughly 80 percent of the consequences come from 20 percent of causes. If you apply that to your relationships, the top 20 percent of your relationships bring you 80 percent of your happiness and joy. Inversely, the bottom 20 percent bring 80 percent of your negative thoughts and emotions.

So, consider the people who regularly steal your time and leave you with more negative than positive feelings—the ones who bring you down and never inspire you or cheer you on. You would almost certainly benefit from dialing back the time you spend with them. If you identify the bottom 20 percent of your relationships and phase them out, you just might find that 80 percent of your interpersonal negativity disappears.

Sounds harsh, I know, but you know what else is harsh? Feeling that you haven't lived the life you wanted to live because of *someone else*. Don't let that happen to you.

WORK

Speaking of things that take and don't give, what about your job? We know, you've got to work for a living—we do too. But if your job is making you miserable on a consistent basis, *change it*. In the experience-rich life you're building, your job should be an asset that contributes to your wealth daily. We spend an average of 90,000 hours at work, equating to one-third of our lives.[17] So, if at all possible, you might as well make work something you enjoy.

You might be able to make your existing job better by collaborating with your employer to change certain aspects of it. Maybe you need to switch roles, adjust your schedule, or transfer to a different location. Maybe you want more responsibility and challenge. Maybe you need to get away from a toxic boss or teammates. If small changes could make a big difference, don't wait around—ask if they're possible.

But sometimes those adjustments aren't possible or aren't enough, in which case, it's time for a new job. It's not a crazy proposition. People do it all the time. Polish your resume, get on LinkedIn, and check out job postings. Want to start your own business? Do the research. Can you take out a loan? Any potential partners? Know anyone who might invest in you? Ask. Shamelessly.

None of this is easy, it's true. When work becomes a time thief, the problem might not get solved overnight—but the sooner you start talking to people and making moves, the sooner your path forward will become clear. And if you do that, you might be surprised at what happens. I sure was.

After my bankruptcy, even with multiple jobs and my new training business, I was still living check to check. Turns out it's expensive to live in Los Angeles. And dating, while not impossible, was much harder with a perpetually empty bank account.

Seeing the success of my personal training business, I wondered if there were more things I could do to make money around my passions. I had always loved cool graphic tees and had worn them religiously since I was in charge of my own wardrobe. I had taken a screen printing class my freshman year of high school, which I grossly misinterpreted to mean that I was qualified to be a fashion designer. So, I persuaded an old high school friend to start an apparel brand with me, beginning with a line of high-end graphic tees. We paid a freelancer to spin our SoCal inspiration (punk rock, Mexico, surf) into designs, mailed glossy mockups in nice envelopes (that was how you did it then) to men's clothing boutiques all over the country, and actually managed to get orders from a couple dozen stores within a month. We rushed off to downtown LA factories to get our product made and become the next Dolce & Gabbana.

We decided we needed a small warehouse for our new "successful" venture, so we found an old 1,000-square-foot warehouse in an industrial part of town and signed a one-year lease. We only needed about a tenth of that space, but we justified it by saying we would build a skateboard ramp to use while we grew into it. Win-win.

Within a few weeks, another friend suddenly needed some space to warehouse and ship out the first batch of products for his small footwear company. He offered to pay for the service if we agreed to be his shipping warehouse for the next six months. Sure, we said—the skate ramp could wait. Another friend heard about the arrangement and asked for the same deal for his small apparel brand. Answer: sure.

This trend continued for the next three years, including moving twice into bigger buildings to accommodate the shipping company that was growing out of our not-really-growing apparel brand. Eventually, we decided to shut down the apparel brand and focus on the shipping business, which grew over the next seven years to over 100 employees and eight figures in revenue.

By that point, we were on track to have far more financial success than I could have ever imagined, and I was extremely proud of what we had built. But as the business grew, I increasingly found myself working around the clock to ensure its survival. I had solved my money problems, but I had begun to neglect the other important things in my life. My recent marriage, my personal relationships outside of work, and my health all started to deteriorate. I was eating poorly and barely sleeping. Not only was there *still* no skate ramp, I wasn't skating *at all* anymore. Or doing much of anything else I enjoyed.

It had all been great. Until it wasn't. I had burned myself out.

Things aren't always what they seem, and this was when I started to question how I was measuring success. The whole reason we wound up with the "successful" shipping business was the "failed" clothing line. But in the three years running that clothing line, I was rewarded with rich first-time experiences like press tours in Japan and Hong Kong; business trips to New York and Seattle to meet with Bloomingdales, Saks, and Nordstrom; travel across the US to visit cool boutiques; long days and longer nights at trade shows and their iconic, over-the-top brand parties; and friendships with actors, musicians, and athletes who were fans of the brand.

The successful shipping company gave me financial security, which is no small matter. But it also gave me a great deal of stress and very few of those rich experiences I had briefly experienced with the apparel brand. A typical day meant leaving for work at 5 a.m., driving in traffic for two hours, working for 12 hours, then driving home in traffic for two more hours—and questions were starting to bubble up to the surface. One night, after a particularly exhausting day, I sat down at my kitchen table and wrote out the first questions that would eventually become the Treasure Map exercise. What was I doing it all for? Was this how I wanted to spend my life? Or even the next five to 10 years?

The answer was a hard *No.* The results were enlightening, powerful, and scary. I was grateful and proud to have built something from the ground up, provided myself with a stable income, and given jobs and benefits to others. But, as much as building the shipping company had provided an incredibly valuable experience, I knew it wasn't how I wanted to spend the rest of my days.

This was right when my dad became ill for the last time. I truly believe that my dad rested easy when his time came because of the decisions he had made to change his life. Seeing that brought deep clarity to me regarding my own future.

It forced me to put my life back under the microscope. What did I really care about? What really mattered? What did I want to be remembered for?

It became obvious that one thing mattered most to me: what I could do for others. It sounded cliché (and still does), but I wanted to do something that made the world a better place. Not at the end, like some billionaire CEO turned philanthropist. I wanted to do something that changed lives every day and every step of the way.

Thanks to my dad's example, I knew I had zero excuses for not starting now. With just $100 a month (of his whopping

$716), he had started a charity for educating local kids where he lived in Mexico. Actually, when it started, it wasn't even a charity—it was just one family with six kids, living in an actual landfill. He saw their need and decided to help buy groceries for them.

But then his friends heard and wanted to pitch in to help more struggling families in the same situation. Soon, it grew into a whole operation, with a board of directors and everything. The earliest beneficiaries were little kids when this started, and they've graduated from college now. Hundreds more have received scholarships, school supplies, and more to lift them and their families out of abject poverty. My dad hardly had any disposable income, but he decided to help one family, and that turned into a movement that outlived him and has helped many more people than he ever dreamed.

So, if I knew that what would matter most in the end for me was what I did to make the world a better place, why was I not working on that every single day?

When I asked myself that question, my whole approach to life changed. I sold my shares in the shipping company and walked away, toward something more impactful...and that eventually led to me starting LSTN with Bridget.

Do I regret it? No way. I knew I had gotten all the value I could out of building and running the shipping company. To stay would have been to willfully put off what my heart was telling me to do with my life. I traded 10 years of predictably profitable yet unfulfilling work for 10 financially risky years of joyful adventure, doing charity work in countries all over the world.

From Impossible to Improbable to Inevitable

The beginning of any great adventure is ripe with a thousand possible futures.

From juvenile delinquent to high school graduate, independent contractor to bankruptcy, personal training out of my garage to CEO of an eight-figure business with over 100 employees, the experiences I had along the way were some of the best and most valuable experiences in my life. Each step of the way started with an idea and plenty of great excuses for why it wouldn't work, and why I shouldn't do it. Don't listen to your excuses—follow your heart and start taking radical responsibility for your own life.

✦ ✦ ✦

EXERCISES

Time and Money

Our experiences aren't just wants, they are actual needs, and as such, we need to allocate resources for them accordingly. This means both our time and our money.

These exercises prove that you can meaningfully change the quality of your life without making big sacrifices or hitting the pause button on your normal existence.

TIME TRACKING

Time is our most valuable resource. Yet, research shows that when people try to retrospectively estimate how they spend their time, they can be pretty far off the mark. To get to the truth, you need to track your time as you're spending it. It's the best way to arrest time thieves and put them behind bars.

1. Set up a time tracking tool. There are many free apps, but you could also use your calendar or even a paper journal (there's a printable version in the resources section of our website). The tool doesn't matter, as long as it gives you a clear and accurate picture of how you use every minute of every day.

2. Track everything you do for five days. We mean it—no guessing, no leaving out the "small" or "silly" stuff. Track it all.

3. Add up all the time you spent in each distinct activity—work, sleep, cooking, grooming, transportation, social media, television, errands, childcare, exercise, hobbies, all of it. After you do this, add up all the buckets and find out how much time you really have.

4. Does anything surprise you? Do your actions align with your stated priorities? Is your "free" time going toward things you've intentionally chosen and genuinely want to do, or is it getting stolen and squandered?

EXPERIENCE ALLOWANCE

When you were younger, you might have had some type of allowance to use on whatever you wanted. What if you gave yourself an allowance for your experiences? We're not personal finance experts, and there are plenty of books on that if you want to go deep (*I Will Teach You To Be Rich* by Ramit Sethi is a great place to start). We do, however, know that when experiences truly become the priority, spending habits often change.

1. Make a list of experiences you want to have but have been putting off for financial reasons. Figure out how much each one costs so you have concrete savings goals.

2. Create a place to set aside money that's just for those experiences. It can be a piggy bank at home or an actual bank account. Some banks even offer virtual savings "buckets" that allow you to collect money for specific goals without opening a separate account.

3. Look closely at your expenses. Look for items that aren't strictly necessary, or where you may be spending more than you need to. Compare those expenses to the experiences on your list from Step 1. Which are more important to you? Maybe you could make coffee at home instead of picking up a latte every morning. Maybe you only need one streaming subscription instead of four. Maybe you could opt for a romantic picnic at the park instead of a swanky restaurant.

4. Whatever you cut from your previous spending now goes toward experiences. If taking your lunch to work instead of buying it saves you $50 a week, put $50 a week into your experience allowance. If you think about buying a $30 shirt but then decide to prioritize experiences instead, save $30 toward those experiences.

Note: Please go to ExperientialBillionaire.com *for an in-depth worksheet on how to assess your current income and expenses to determine your experiences budget.*

Chapter Four

THE CAVE YOU FEAR TO ENTER HOLDS THE TREASURE YOU SEEK

“Expose yourself to
your deepest fear;
after that, fear has
no power, and the
fear of freedom
shrinks and vanishes.
You are free.”

—Jim Morrison

Bridget:

I stood side stage at the Ace Hotel's theater in downtown Los Angeles. Peering out, I saw hundreds of reporters and attendees staring up at a man who had made billions disrupting the music and airline industries, bought tropical islands, crossed *both* the Pacific and Atlantic oceans in a hot air balloon, gone to outer space, founded over 100 companies, and generously gave back while doing all of that. A rebel who rose to the top without a fancy degree or inheritance, just big dreams and the gumption to go after them. Someone who I aspired to be.

Sir Richard Branson.

As I took in the enormity of this moment, my hero looked toward me waiting in the wings and said, "And welcome Bridget Hilton, a truly inspiring woman who really is making business an adventure." I walked across the gorgeous stage to roars of clapping and cameras flashing. Several of my friends beamed up at me from the audience and looked on in admiration as I sat down next to my grinning idol for a fireside chat.

It was the wet dream of any entrepreneur.

There was only one problem. A big one.

I was absolutely *terrified* of public speaking. When I was a kid and we had to take turns reading from the textbook in class, I used to count the number of students before me to skip ahead and practice what I'd need to read. In elementary school, I'd play roles such as "tree" in the school play to avoid having any lines. I dreaded even going to the front of the classroom to sharpen a pencil. In my first office job, I never got up the nerve to speak in a meeting—and when forced, my face turned beet red. I once had to present a music video to a big group of colleagues and nearly had a panic attack the night before. As an entrepreneur, sometimes conferences or companies would ask me to come speak, and every single time, I'd make up an excuse for why I couldn't go. Once, I even faked a death in the family to get out of an event.

Turns out I wasn't alone. Glossophobia, or a fear of public speaking, is believed to affect up to 75 percent of the population. Several studies show that public speaking is the number one fear, even over *death* (and spiders!).[18] Yikes.

And yet five years prior, when LSTN was still running out of my dining room, Joe and I went through the Treasure Map exercise for the first time. An item on my list? Have a beer with Sir Richard Branson—a dream that seemed so audacious at the time that I laughed as I wrote it down. I didn't even consider how I'd react if it actually happened.

So, even though it had made my palms sweat and my heart drop when I was invited to speak there, I said yes. He was my hero, after all. I had to overcome my fear to make this happen.

Thankfully, the moderator had sent me a list of questions ahead of time. What a relief. I stayed up all night, memorized them all, and prepared slam dunk answers and funny anecdotes in front of my mirror. That small comfort was probably the only reason I managed to actually get my ass on stage.

But the moderator must have lost her notes, or maybe she had a secret vendetta against me, because she didn't ask a single question I had prepared for. I totally bombed and drew blanks, my heart leaping out of my chest the whole time. Cue the cold sweats. I basically blacked out.

At least, that's what I thought was happening—no one else seemed to notice anything unusual. In fact, I'm pretty sure no one even cared about what I had to say at all. Richard said incredibly kind things, the crowd was charmed by his charisma, and I got to live out a dream.

Afterward, I did end up getting that beer with him (several, actually, judging from the photos from that night). We bonded over our shared experiences of giving hearing to those in need, a cause he was also passionate about. I confessed that I was terrified during the whole event, and I was shocked when he told me he was terrified of public speaking, too. But he loved that it helped others learn from his journey and mistakes along the way, so instead of doing rehearsed speeches that added pressure, he now just speaks from the heart and imagines that he's having a chat with a friend instead of a giant room.

I thought about all the times I'd had opportunities to speak at events and the voice in my head said, "You don't deserve this," or, "You don't really want to do this," or, "You can't do this." I had given that voice free rein, allowing it to convince me to give up on the idea of speaking altogether. I felt like I was always on the edge of being exposed as a fraud. After speaking with Sir Richard, I realized the voice in my head had been wrong.

To hear that someone insanely accomplished felt that way gave me hope for myself. It wasn't just beginners like me. I could remember that for the next time I felt nervous on stage—that we're all human. And it would be okay.

At the afterparty later that evening, members of the crowd came up and told me they were inspired by the story of LSTN, and that they had spent the last few hours thinking of what they could do to help others. One attendee told me they had already set up a meeting at their company headquarters to brainstorm how to integrate social good into their business. Another said they made plans to take their kids to volunteer at a shelter that upcoming weekend. It was the first time I wondered if maybe I should do this more often—it seemed to be resonating with people.

Until then, I had thought my impact would be purely through the act of giving hearing. I had never considered that I could amplify my impact by simply speaking about those experiences. If I could be deeply present and share these stories with a room, it could potentially lead to others giving in ways they hadn't considered before. In a way, it seemed selfish to let my anxiety get in the way of a possible domino effect.

This was a crossroads—I could go for something big and do something bigger than myself, or I could retreat into my fear.

When I thought about it that way, the right choice was clear. My lifelong phobia had to go. So, I put together a plan and took the first baby steps. I put goals on the calendar and visualized speaking in front of thousands of people. I started outlining a keynote speech. I downloaded an app that helped me with pace and my "umms" and "uhhs." I made my accountability buddies read and listen to my talk. I filmed myself speaking and reviewed the videos (terribly painful). I gave my speech to a wall while blasting metal music to distract me. I still regularly walk down the beach while reciting it out loud (and get a lot of concerned looks thrown my way).

As I became more serious about it, I hired a brutally honest coach to tell me what was and wasn't working. I joined a community of speakers who gave me a safe space to voice my highs and lows along the journey. All of these gave me the confidence to push past my fear. Now, just a few years later, speaking is my passion and livelihood. The cave I feared to enter held the treasure I was seeking.

I bet the same is true for you. What are you afraid to do? What makes you so uncomfortable that you avoid it? Maybe you know you're afraid, or maybe you make up other explanations: you're bad at it, or you don't deserve it, or it isn't worth the effort. Those little lies soothe the ego, but the fear they mask is still there, holding you back.

We need to think—and act—differently about fear. You'll see that it can actually be a guide to follow, not a monster to avoid like the plague. It can lead you to bigger, better, more meaningful experiences that shape your life in the best way.

Fear Doesn't Always Tell the Truth

Fear is a biological response. When your brain interprets information as a threat, whether that's a real threat in the environment or a negative thought, it triggers the amygdala, the emotional epicenter of your brain. That initiates a chemical cascade of stress hormones, creating physiological responses in your body. Your heart rate and breathing get faster. Blood rushes away from your head and core, moving to oxygenate and mobilize your major muscle groups. You might sweat, shiver, or choke up. Your mouth might feel dry. You might feel dizzy. Your mind seems to go blank.

This uncomfortable feeling is actually millions of years of evolution at work, trying desperately to save your ass through the magic of the fight-or-flight response. Your system is trying to ready you to do whatever it takes to keep you safe. We need this system. When we're in actual danger, it helps us do things we could otherwise hardly imagine—we've all heard stories of people exhibiting superhuman strength or courage in a crisis, like a bystander lifting a car off of a trapped driver after an accident, or a mother fighting off an attacking animal to save her child.

These days, though, most situations we face do not require lifesaving efforts. Now our amygdala is most often triggered by thoughts that aren't actually a threat to our physical safety. *What will people think if I try this and blow it? What if I can't actually do this? What if I fail? What if they judge me?*

This kind of fear doesn't empower you. It holds you hostage. It's why people won't leave the job that they hate, or won't go to parties, or won't travel...all because this fight-or-flight system tells them they're in danger when they're not.

Many times, the fight-or-flight response gets triggered by your imagination alone—not anything that's actually happening, just your negative predictions of the future. They can be "what if" thoughts or all-or-nothing beliefs like "I'll never be able to get that job" or "I'll always be afraid of public speaking." You're fortune telling and expecting the worst, which activates your fear and can lead you to make choices that undermine your goals.

In our survey, we asked 20,000 people to tell us about the fears keeping them from their dreams. Here's what they said:

> "I'm afraid to sign up for the half marathon in my city because I don't know if I can get in good enough shape." —Mark, St. Louis

> "My dream is to be a professional photographer, but I don't feel that I'm good enough to show my photos to anyone else." —Lydia, Orlando

> "I want to do stand-up comedy, but I'm deathly afraid of people not laughing at my jokes." —Rick, Chicago

"I have always wanted to have my own bed and breakfast, but I'm scared that my family will judge me for quitting my career that I worked so hard for." —Claire, Providence

"I want to go on a long European trip by myself, but I'm scared of being all alone." —Laurie, Omaha

These people are so wrapped in imagined negative outcomes that they choose not to even make the attempt. The biological fear response keeps them focused on the potential losses, so they don't consider the possible gains or the true likelihood of each outcome. Your fear wants to protect you... but what about the harm of not going for your dreams? When you think about your ambitions, what are the anxious predictions or "what if" thoughts and fears that come to mind?

Here's Your Permission Slip

When you were a kid, you needed permission for everything. Permission from your parents to watch TV, permission from the teacher to go to the bathroom. Raise your hand, get in line, wait your turn. Obviously, that goes away as you get older...but maybe not entirely.

Because many adults act like they're still waiting for permission to do what they actually want, especially when what they want isn't so easy to reach. They tell themselves they can't, for all kinds of reasons. It's not the right time, they're not ready, they're not good enough, it's a silly idea, it's not prudent. No one else around them is doing that kind of thing. It would be selfish or reckless or arrogant to try.

How would you feel if we said right now that *you have permission?*

Here it is, in black and white: your permission slip. You have permission to take an acting class, go to Bangkok, paint a mountain landscape, learn to make Ethiopian food. To ask for a promotion. To try something new. To change. Even to fail.

That last one might be the most powerful. Our culture isn't exactly failure friendly. People are quick to hide their mistakes and slow to admit them, and rarely is anyone applauded for owning their failures. Mistakes and flaws are for ridiculing and punishing, not celebrating.

It's a shame, because failing is how you learn. You might already know the story of how Thomas Edison tried thousands of different materials before he created an electric lightbulb that worked long enough for practical use. As he said, "I have not failed 10,000 times—I've successfully found 10,000 ways that will not work." He understood that each apparent failure was actually a step forward because it gave him more information about what to try next.

The same is true for you as you build your experientially rich life. The goal is not perfection. Our society is so obsessed with perfection that when I was growing up, there was actually a game called Perfection, where if you weren't perfect in a set amount of time, the board literally blew up in your face. What the hell kind of lesson for children is that?! What does perfection even mean? That everything goes swimmingly the first time? That's not perfection—that's just avoiding the big risks and challenges that are actually worth taking on. It's seeking false comfort in, well, the comfortable.

When you give yourself permission to fail, you're getting permission to try—to take shots, work hard, get creative, and get back up when you fall down. Do you want to start a podcast? Be willing to have no one listen to it. Do you want to join a soccer team? Be willing to be the worst player on the team. Do you want to be featured in an art show? Be willing to have your art rejected by the curator.

It all amounts to putting aside your ego. It's learning that to fail is not to be a failure, and when you toss that label in the garbage where it belongs, you can open unexpected doors for yourself.

We were reminded of that in a massive way as we flew to Beijing a few years ago. Our LSTN coworkers were with us on the way to a trade show. As we looked around the cabin at people of all races, young and old, they all had one thing in common: they were wearing our product, thanks to our partnership with Delta Air Lines.

My jet-lagged, half-in-the-bag self filled with pride as I looked down row after row to see the logo I had designed in my apartment years earlier. It begged the question many had asked us: How did such a small company get a contract with the biggest airline in the world?

Like many of my favorite stories, it all started at a party. A friend of a friend happened to be an executive at Delta Air

Lines. A casual conversation about LSTN's mission intrigued him, and he immediately pulled out his phone to buy a pair of headphones, mostly because he was (and still is) a nice guy. He loved them, and we started talking about what we could do together.

If we had compared our six-person start-up, with its tiny office and almost-empty bank account, to an airline with 80,000 employees, we never would have tried to pull this partnership off. We waited in the lobby for our scheduled pitch meeting, knowing that executives from Bose, Sony, and Beats would go in before us—companies with private jets, 10-figure market caps, and ads with professional athletes all over TV. If we had asked ourselves whether we were good enough or ready for this opportunity, we would have given up right then.

Instead, we put our egos aside and our hearts on our sleeves. After three years of negotiations (yes, it took that long), we landed the contract to supply millions of headphones for Delta Air Lines. We signed a deal for more money than I had ever even imagined seeing...and then we promptly gave it all away. One hundred percent of the proceeds went to charity because we wanted to make a real, lasting impact from the partnership.

That financial decision snowballed into a mountain of experiences we will never forget. To announce the partnership, Delta produced an epic commercial spotlighting two of our patients in Peru, young brothers who could now hear thanks to LSTN and the Starkey Hearing Foundation.

Taking them around Arequipa with us and a film crew was an adventure in itself, and through the commercial, their story received millions of views and touched countless lives. One Delta executive who was onsite during filming was so moved that she decided to dedicate the rest of her life to philanthropic causes. Another pledged their commitment to doubling down on the airline giant's giving initiatives. Who knows how many acts of kindness and giving flowed from their generosity.

That commercial sparked a chain reaction of new experiences. It took us to an awards stage where Joe and I gave a speech right between Ben Affleck and Aerosmith—talk about imposter syndrome. We cohosted the first ever silent disco at 30,000 feet with our favorite DJ, Questlove (now "Oscar winner, Questlove"). We threw a launch party with some of our favorite Los Angeles chefs, Jon and Vinny.

All this happened because we *went for it.* Even though it was scary, even though it was a long shot, even though it would have seemed safer to listen to that inner critic asking, "Who are you to think you belong here?" We didn't let less important things distract us from the goal, even during the years of negotiations. We didn't let our fragile egos dissuade us from going up against much, *much* bigger competitors.

We wanted it, so we did what it took to make it happen. Instead of letting the prospect of a bad outcome hold us back, we asked, "What's the best that could happen?" Now we don't have to wonder what might have been if we'd taken that leap.

What can you give yourself permission to do?

Fear Is an Invitation to Evolve

When you're in fight-or-flight mode, everything you do or don't do teaches the brain something about the perceived threat. When you avoid or flee the situation, your brain experiences a wave of relief. The amygdala learns that avoiding that situation is how you stay safe from that threat.

This is exactly how you want the brain to respond if the threat is a grizzly bear. But what if the perceived threat is something less biologically adaptive, like a worry about being judged or teased? Let's say you're invited to a party full of new people, and you have thoughts of looking dumb, making a mistake, or being judged. The fear response is triggered, and you decide not to go to the party. Whew! Relief! You don't have to be judged!

However, you've now taught the brain that parties are dangerous (even the ones without tequila), and avoiding them is how you stay safe. The next time you have to attend a party or event, the anxiety response is even stronger—the brain desperately tries to get you to flee, because that's how you've stayed safe in the past.

Anxiety gets worse and worse as you avoid it and can even start to generalize. A fear of parties can spread to all social events, and then to brief interactions with baristas at the coffee shop. It can become debilitating, preventing you from doing things you really want to do. That's what happens when you train your brain to sound the alarm when there's no real danger.

However, let's say you choose to behave differently when you're anxious but not in real danger. You recognize your fear, accept it, and go to the party anyway. In fact, you go to a lot of parties, even though your fight-or-flight response kicks in.

The brain is collecting data about what happens and soon realizes, *Wait a minute, nothing bad is happening! Maybe this isn't actually dangerous!* Over time, you retrain your amygdala about what is safe, and the fear response becomes less intense or disappears.

If you sit around waiting to feel comfortable, you'll be waiting forever. Your brain won't magically retrain itself. You have to act *before* it feels comfortable, before you feel ready. You can choose to do things that scare you—to feel the fear and act anyway. Avoiding your fears makes your world smaller; facing them expands it.

Maybe you can't relate to the party anxiety scenario, but I bet there is at least one area in your life where you are afraid to fail. It could be your work, your finances, your relationships, your body, your reputation, your legacy...there are many possibilities. We all have something we're afraid to ruin, and that fear holds us back from taking that very thing to the next level.

With the right training, your brain can unlearn its fear of virtually anything, even things you would think are unquestionable...like lions.

Joe and I were in Kenya on a philanthropic mission in the Maasai community, the perfect chance to fulfill our dream of going on a safari. The morning after the mission work concluded, we woke up before sunrise to hit the plains. It was a rugged outfit, riding around the Serengeti in doorless Land Cruisers trying to get close to elephants and big cats.

And we did—a little too close, actually.

It had been pouring rain through the night and the ground had turned into a few feet of mud. We were attempting to get our tires unstuck when our guide said in a hushed but urgent tone, "*Don't. Move. Be. Quiet.*"

On the right side of the car, a giant lioness with the drooling jaw of a cold-blooded killer was walking directly toward me. There was nothing between us but three feet of air—not even a car door. In this much scarier version of The Lion King, Nala crouched, we locked eyes, and I felt her slink past my legs just as we were able to peel out from the mud. My life flashed before me as I pissed my pants and imagined my obituary reading, "In death, Bridget became what she loved most in life: a delicious meal." *Hakuna matata.*

We thought the mega cat's demon stare was the true embodiment of fear, but we hadn't quite seen it all yet. Later that afternoon, we were inching through the tall grass, looking for signs of life, when we saw a figure coming toward us in the distance. It didn't look like an animal, but there were no roads or villages in that direction for miles and miles. Still, 20 minutes later, a Maasai woman appeared, her traditional bright red and blue patterned Shuka standing out starkly against the endless brownish-green grass.

We were stunned. It was 100 degrees with no water in sight, and we were in a vast, open valley. We expected to see giant cats in this area at any moment, and she was just waltzing through? And what was she carrying on her back? Wait... was that a *baby*?

She walked up to us and we chatted. I told her about our close encounter with the lion and said incredulously, "Aren't you scared of the lions while you're walking all by yourself?"

She laughed at me and said, "No. I am only afraid of the hippos."

The Maasai know from experience that lions are lazy and unlikely to attack humans unless they feel threatened. (They certainly could have fooled me.) On the other hand, hippos (yes, the giant water-pigs) are highly aggressive and kill more people each year than lions, elephants, leopards, buffalo, and rhinos combined. Hungry, hungry hippos indeed.

So there you go—even the things that seem genuinely worth fearing might not be what they seem. More often than not, the more you understand something, the less scary it becomes.

Don't Fear the Other

"Cow blood. Cow meat. And cow milk."

That's what a Maasai warrior told me when I asked what they liked to eat. "Wait...that's it?!" I exclaimed. "Yes—it's very good, very simple," he said with a laugh. As I admired his muscles glistening in the sun, I took a sip (not bad!) and briefly contemplated switching my diet before remembering the extremely low chances of the granola health stores back home in LA selling bulk cow blood.

On the surface, the Maasai people could hardly be more different from me. Our attire, what we eat, our daily activities, our language, our surroundings, our communities—we seem to have nothing in common. But the more time I spent with them, the more I realized how untrue this was.

This warrior welcomed us into his village with genuine hospitality. We found common ground in music, my first love and a huge part of their culture. They taught us their traditional songs and dances and told us that contemporary Tanzanian and Kenyan hip-hop artists often incorporated Maasai rhythms into their songs. The women of the tribe showed us how they make the gorgeous jewelry they sell to tourists. We made a fire together, had a jumping contest (I lost miserably), and listened to exciting tales of life in the bush. Yes, we are different on the surface, but when it comes to values, we share more than I ever expected. We love music, our community, the outdoors, and being entrepreneurs. And a juicy steak, of course.

As human beings, it's simply in our nature to draw a line between "us" and "them"—our people and other people. "Other" people are the ones we don't understand or relate to, and we're much more likely to perceive them as scary or threatening, whether they really are or not. We see this repeated endlessly throughout history, all over the world, and it continues today.

The solution to this fear is simple: get closer. The better you know people, the harder it is to demonize them.

I learned this again and again as I traveled to all 50 of the United States. It was a project I started taking seriously in 2016, after the presidential election left the country feeling more divided than ever. By then, I'd had a pretty solid head start, between childhood road trips and being on tour in the music industry. I decided to make an effort to get at least a taste of all the rest—maybe that way I would have a better idea of what "land of the free" really meant.

Traveling the US feels like you're visiting a bunch of different countries wrapped into one. Downtown Seattle has little in common with a cornfield town in Kansas. When someone from a different country thinks of the US, they likely think of NYC or Hollywood or Silicon Valley. The reality is that the country is classified as 95 percent rural—there's a *ton* of wide-open space. And in all that space is an incredible diversity of landscapes, lifestyles, ethnicities, languages, and beliefs. Sadly, it's estimated that half of Americans see fewer than 10 states in their lifetimes.

In every state, I made an effort to experience its unique culture—its traditional foods, special places in nature, and signature activities. I ate hatch chiles and went hot air ballooning over the Rio Grande in New Mexico, worked on a lobster boat in Massachusetts, ate reindeer and went on a midnight glacier hike in Alaska, visited Native American reservations in the Dakotas, rolled down sand dunes in Indiana, ate beignets and watched jazz in New Orleans, roped steers in Wyoming, and ended my quest by eating Spam musubi and learning beekeeping in Hawaii.

In each place, I made an effort to speak to people who seemed to be on opposite sides of the spectrum than me in many ways. I saw more truck stops, tumbleweeds, and roadside dive bars than I ever thought possible. It was a far cry from what the news would have you believe. I found that if you watch the news, it's easy to worry about this country... but there are some things that can't be learned through a screen. They must be seen, heard, and felt in person. If you drive through the States, there's beauty to be found in each place—both in the landscapes and the people.

After all those experiences, it's much easier to see that everyone has their reasons for thinking and living the way they do. Most people aren't crazy or evil—they've just arrived at a particular set of conclusions based on the experiences they've had and the information they've been given. I'm now a firm believer that most people are just friends we haven't met yet, as the vast majority of people across the United States (and the world, for that matter) were fundamentally friendly and helpful. When you recognize that, you can do away with the labels and fear and just listen to each other with empathy and open minds (hey, a girl can dream!).

So, Why Not?

Ultimately, the only opinion that matters is your own. Why not write that book? Why not learn to play the piano? Why not get your boating license? When you master your own ego and stop worrying about the judgment of others and potential negative outcomes, fear can evaporate, and you'll be surprised by how fast the voice of dissuasion disappears.

✦ ✦ ✦

EXERCISE

Everything You Want Is On the Other Side of Fear

What's one specific thing that fear is holding you back from going after? For example, here are some common ones:

- Traveling to a new country
- Taking a new job or trying a new career
- Moving to a new city
- Learning or using a new skill
- Committing to a romantic relationship
- Making new friends/socializing

Focus on that one fear and answer the following questions:

1. If you did what you're afraid to do, what negative things might happen?

2. What would be so bad about that? What would it mean about you if your fear came true?

3. What does this tell you about what you believe about your safety, worth, competence, or lovability?

4. Where did you learn to believe this about yourself?

5. How does this belief keep you from pursuing your dreams?

6. What would you do if you believed something different about yourself?

Note: Go to ExperientialBillionaire.com *for an extended version of this exercise, developed in collaboration with anxiety expert Kristen Salvatore, LMSW from the University of Michigan.*

Chapter Five

MAKE SOMEDAY TODAY

"You can't cross the sea merely by standing and staring at the water."

—Rabindranath Tagore

Joe:

After I sold my shares in the shipping company, I took a few months off for the first time in, well, ever. On paper, things looked great. After a decade of running a business, my mind was finally clear and calm, and I was getting my health back. I was married and ready to start a family, something I had always wanted and was excited about. Financially, I was in the best place I had ever been—I could finally afford to pay my bills on time and eat out when I wanted. I was ready to tackle my next big entrepreneurial adventure: a business with a humanitarian purpose right at its core.

Instead, my life deteriorated into a stereotypical country song. My dad had only passed a few months earlier. Then, my four-year-old dog died unexpectedly. Then I got divorced. Dad died, dog died, wife left...yep. I was just a few twangy guitar chords away from a hit single.

Those curve balls had me hitting pause on all my planning. My inner voice said, "You're going through a lot right now. Just wait until it's a better time to start something new. You can always dip into your newfound savings and put things on pause for a year. Or two. Better yet, why not wait until you have some real inspiration?"

The temptation worked. My momentum stalled. I waited.

If you spend any time around kids, you know they *hate* to wait for the things they want. They're the ones in the back of the car asking, "Are we there yet?" When you say you'll do something "soon," they want to know *when.* If they see something they want, they don't think, *Oh, maybe I'll come back for that later.* They want it *now.*

As we grow up, we learn to be patient. We get better at delaying gratification, which is important, because no one wants to see a grown man throw a tantrum in the grocery store. And, of course, most big rewards in life take time. We have to put in the effort now to get a payoff later. That's true in school, work, and anytime you're building a new skill or working toward a big goal.

But maybe we get a little too good at putting off our desires. We go from saying "gimme now" to "maybe someday." Someday we'll visit that dream destination, someday we'll get back in shape, someday we'll learn a foreign language, or start a garden, or play in a band. That's what I was doing. I told myself I would start that social impact business...someday.

Well, bad news: Someday is not a day on the calendar.

It's a ruse. A trick we play on ourselves. A way to avoid confronting the fact that if we don't do something, "not right now" will become "never." An illusion that makes us think we have more time and always will. We tell ourselves we'll do things "someday" and then make no plans whatsoever to actually do them. Then, sadly, we just never get around to doing them.

This is the dreaded Someday Syndrome, and it's an epidemic. Almost every grown-up picks up this perverse addiction without even noticing, and most never kick it. We know this because studies consistently show that most people's top regrets aren't things they wish they hadn't done; they're things *they wanted to do but never did*. In our survey of over 20,000 people, three out of four listed something they hadn't done as their number one regret in life. Here are a few examples from participants aged 65+.

> "I always wanted to buy a motorhome and spend a year driving around the country with my late wife." —Sam, St. Louis

> "I regret not going to nursing school. That was something I felt passionately about that I never pursued and now it's too late." —Louisa, Lexington

> "I wish I would have spent more time with my two boys when they were growing up instead of always working." —Paul, Phoenix

> "I regret staying with my husband when I knew it wasn't the right thing to do for me, but I felt pressured by society into staying." —Kathy, Park City

> "It was my dream from childhood to fly a plane. But now my eyes are too bad. I will always regret not doing that." —Thomas, New Orleans

> "I greatly regret that I didn't ask my parents more about their lives growing up while I still had them." —Donald, Spokane

"I won extensive awards in high school for my artistic ability and regret not pursuing that God-given talent." —Sherri, Denver

"I wish I would have taken my son down south to Mississippi where I grew up before he passed away." —Gabriel, Nashville

"I didn't have the guts to start my own landscaping company when I had the chance, and that is the biggest regret of my life." —David, Charlotte

We all have regrets for things we've done that maybe didn't work out as planned. That's okay. As life goes on, those regrets will begin to look minor in comparison to the regrets you feel for the things you never tried. To avoid those big regrets, take a cue from the kids in the back of the car: stop taking "someday" for an answer.

Action Is the Anti-Regret

If we know most people's biggest regrets are the things they haven't done, it becomes clear that our greatest enemy is inaction. In those first few months after my life fell apart, I didn't know what to do...so I did nothing. I waited for the pain to pass, telling myself I needed time to heal before I could move forward. I waited for clarity, hoping answers would magically reveal themselves to me.

They didn't. Instead, the seeds of regret started growing. I could feel them in the pit of my stomach, getting bigger with each passing day.

I wasn't regretting the losses I had experienced. Yes, they were agonizing and difficult to process, but I also felt fortunate, in a way. I had been lucky enough to have a dad and know him well. Lucky enough to have been (mostly) happily married for a number of years. Lucky enough to have the means and live in a place where I could have a dog as a companion.

The regret was coming from the things that *weren't* happening. My dream of building a new business at the intersection of fashion and philanthropy wasn't materializing. All the urgency and clarity from my dad's death had trickled away, replaced by indecision and paralysis.

I knew if I wanted to make the world a better place, each day I delayed was wasted. Not just wasted—*lost* forever. But I didn't know where to start, so I kept waiting. I wallowed in that feeling for months before I realized I had it all backwards.

In fact, I already knew how to tackle this ambitious dream. I had navigated tough challenges and scary life transitions before: overcoming addiction and graduating high school on time, moving to the beach with strangers, starting a business. Those all started as big, nebulous ideas, too. They only became real when I started actually *doing something*.

So, I made my social enterprise start-up to-do list: business license, bank account, website, business plan, launch partner materials, software setup, and on and on. I captured every step I could think of, then organized and prioritized them. Each one went on the calendar, forming a clear timeline to a specific launch date. To create accountability for myself, I announced that launch date to everyone I knew—friends, family, business partners, and even potential press and PR outlets.

And guess what? My funk lifted. With each step I took, I gained momentum. The more I did, the more ideas I had. The more progress I made, the clearer the way forward became. Everything didn't go exactly to plan, of course. It never does. Perspective changes as you take steps, no matter the direction. But even a step backward after making a wrong turn is a step in the right direction. And once I was in motion, it was easy to stay that way—I just adapted the plan when necessary and kept going. Getting started was the hardest part.

Within a few months of taking my first steps, I had a real, functioning company called This Helps that designed and sold shoes, shirts, hats, and accessories, and we used the proceeds from each item sold to support philanthropic causes I was passionate about.

Over the course of the next year, I sold tens of thousands of products and traveled the globe to work directly with my new charity partners. I helped install water filtration systems in Haiti, support victims of human trafficking in Indonesia and Cambodia, and build schools in rural Guatemala. I also worked with cancer research organizations, reforestation programs, and animal shelters right here in the US. Along the way, I rode dirt bikes through monkey-filled jungles, organized skydiving charity events, ran a marathon, went river rafting, took salsa and cooking classes, went paragliding, and drank with the locals in many remote and unfamiliar locations.

That year was the first time I felt I was truly living my ideal self, and it sparked a chain reaction that completely reshaped my life. Those experiences helped me heal from the traumatic ones that had happened at the beginning of the year. Because of those experiences, I ended up meeting Bridget and co-founding LSTN. That led to meeting my wife, Yasmine, with whom I now have two wonderful children. The trend only continued, the following years full of experiences that exceeded my wildest expectations. I spoke on stage with Trevor Noah in New York City, delivered talks to business leaders in Monaco, shot a commercial with Javier Bardem on a Vancouver rooftop at 3 a.m., flew in helicopters and private jets (not mine, of course), was featured on the local news (look, Mom! It's me!), spoke on a cruise ship full of entrepreneurs in the Bahamas, met incredibly talented and inspiring people that I'm proud to call friends now, and somehow wound up on the front page of newspapers in both Korea and the Dominican Republic.

Everything I am today began with the simple decision to stop waiting for "someday" and just take action.

The same could be true for you. There could be an incredible transformation waiting to happen in your life, if only you take the first step. The rest of this chapter will show you how to take those critical first steps, overcome Someday Syndrome, and start turning your "somedays" into todays. What have you been putting off to "someday" because it feels too big to tackle?

Be a Part of the Eight Percent

Ninety-two percent of New Year's resolutions fail.[19] That's not a very encouraging statistic when you're thinking about making changes in your life, but let's turn it around. Eight percent succeed, and not by accident or chance. How do they do it?

By consistently taking small, achievable steps toward big goals.

The grander your vision, the more easily it falls prey to Someday Syndrome. All those questions to answer, decisions to make, and obstacles to overcome can make you feel paralyzed. You know it will take time, which makes it seem less urgent. The challenges may be bigger than anything you've faced before, which can be overwhelming. It's so tempting to just sit back and pretend it will happen one day, somehow.

Fight that feeling with baby steps. Breaking your dreams down into specific, achievable actions massively boosts your chances of success. You're more likely to take the first step and more likely to follow through to the end.[20]

That's exactly what I did with my business to-do list. Starting a humanitarian business was a massive endeavor, but applying for a business license? I could wrap my head around that. Find the right paperwork, choose a name, pay the fee—it might take a few hours, tops.

When I had to confront big decisions, like what the business would actually do, I broke those down into steps too. First, brainstorm a big list of all the possibilities. Then, choose criteria to evaluate them. Next, research each possibility and apply the evaluation criteria. From there, making a decision was much easier.

Even if the eventual outcomes you want lie years in the future, you can set the gears in motion now. Want to become an amazing drummer? Start practicing today. Want to do a TED Talk? Start outlining ideas immediately. Got a long list of places you want to see? Prioritize them and start planning the first trip now.

In this process, it's crucial to be detailed. It's not helpful to just write down "travel the world" or "learn piano"—you have to decide exactly what that looks like for you. For example, "learn piano" might actually be, "I'll learn one new song a month by practicing for 30 minutes a day, and here is a list of the 12 songs for this year. At the end of the year, on this specific day, I'll give a recital for my friends and family." It's better to say, "I want to build an A-frame cabin in the woods in Minnesota in five years, and this is what I have to start doing now to make that happen," versus, "I want a cabin someday." If shit happens and you end up pushing that specific goal out by an extra year or two, at least it's still on the calendar, not in the bottomless abyss of "someday."

Even seemingly simple experiences often require multiple steps. For example, let's say you want to go to the gym once a week. You have to choose a gym, start your membership, choose classes or plan your workouts, get the right clothes and shoes...you get the picture. Maybe you want to see a live comedy performance. You have to find out who is on tour, decide who you want to see and when, buy tickets, and figure out how to get there. Visit a museum, write a poem, call your mom more often—if you think through exactly how you're going to do it, you're much more likely to follow through.

Most of the time, the hardest part is taking that first step over the starting line.

Your Calendar Holds Your Real Wealth

Your calendar is the fortune teller of your experiential wealth. It shows you exactly how much value you can expect to reap in the coming days and months, right there in front of you. When you look at your calendar and your Treasure Map together, you'll immediately see how much your efforts align with your intentions—or don't.

We say our goals and dreams are important but words don't matter. Our choices matter. Our actions matter. Our calendar doesn't lie.

There's no magic to it. It's just a basic truth: what gets scheduled gets done. In one study, researchers found that when participants specified exactly where and when they would complete an intended activity, a stunning 91 percent of them followed through.[21] Your calendar is an essential tool for increasing your experiential wealth.

When I was feeling stuck and letting regret grow, my calendar was the dead giveaway that things were all wrong. For the first time in a very long time, it was completely empty. I had left the shipping company with a plan to start something else, but until that something was actually on my calendar, it wasn't real. It was just a wish.

If you're thinking you're in the clear because your calendar is full, hold on a minute. A packed calendar can be just as problematic as an empty one, depending on what it's full of. To quote Henry David Thoreau, "It's not enough to be busy; so are the ants. The question is: What are we busy about?" Most busy people are fully booked with urgent needs and other people's demands—lots of meetings, errands, and obligations but little of what they really want in life. The calendar *looks* full, but in terms of valuable experiences, it's actually empty. (This is part of the "I don't have time" fallacy. You do have time—you're just using it for the wrong things.)

You need a new approach to your calendar—an experience-rich approach. The things you most want to experience in life should go on your calendar first, *before* it fills up with other stuff.

Like your endless to-do list. You know: pay the bills, take out the trash, get groceries, schedule your dentist appointment, buy mom a birthday present, finish your presentation for the big meeting...and on and on forever. That's all life maintenance—stuff you *have* to do to keep living, keep your job, and keep a clean home. We're not advising you to skip it. But does any of it mean anything? Are you going to remember it when you're old?

Nope. But if you're not careful, it will take up your whole day, every day. So can work, if you let it. If you give a task a week instead of an hour, it somehow becomes more complicated and time consuming. It's Parkinson's law: work expands to fill the time available.[22]

So, before you schedule anything else, you've got to put the experiences you actually want, even the small ones, onto your calendar. If they're not on your to-do list and not on your calendar, they're nowhere, which means they'll never happen.

Look at your calendar now. This is your "before" picture—what do you see? If it's not full of valuable experiences, don't expect them to appear out of thin air. You have to put them there. That's what living intentionally is all about.

For example, in our *Life Experiences Survey*, thousands of people said that skydiving was one of the top three things they wanted to do in their lifetime.[23] What's interesting is that skydiving isn't really very hard to do. Is it scary? Hell yeah. But it's available in most places and only requires a few hours and a couple hundred dollars. Anyone can manage that, even if it takes a year to save up the money. But most people have it on their mental "someday" list, so they never bother to actually find out what it takes or make a plan to do it.

When I was 19 years old, I wanted to go skydiving. I told three friends, we committed to a day a month later, saved up $120 each working our respective odd jobs, and when the day came, we went skydiving.

I still remember it like it was yesterday. I can feel the butterflies in my stomach as we moved toward the opening, the adrenaline pumping as I grabbed onto the door frame for one last pull, the feeling of tumbling into the open air, the wind on my face, and the noise of it rushing by as I free fell through open space for 60 seconds that felt like 10 minutes.

Those details are locked in my treasure chest of memories forever. How many memories like that do I have for days when my calendar was empty? Not many.

Again, what gets scheduled gets done. Do *you* want to go skydiving? Schedule it for the first Saturday of next month. Make time for your personal goals and enshrine it on your calendar before your days fill up with other, less important things. I promise, it's an experience you'll never forget.

Hold Yourself Accountable

Your calendar can remind you what to do, but it can't make you do it. To maximize your likelihood of following through on your plans, you need something more than the voice in your head saying, "I should do this, even if I don't feel like it right now." You need an accountability system.

Work and school come with these built-in. Someone tells you what to do and when, and there are positive consequences for following through and negative ones for not.

You're held accountable for your actions. So, if you want to get paid or graduate, you do what you're supposed to do.

Your personal life doesn't come with a built-in accountability system, so if you want to make progress, you have to create one yourself. All it takes is the right combination of three simple tools: nudges, self-imposed consequences, and accountability partners.

NUDGES

A nudge is something in your environment that makes it easier to take the right action. It keeps your priorities top of mind and reduces the barriers to executing them. The idea is to design your life so it takes less willpower and energy to do the things you want to do.

Often, a nudge is a physical object. For example, I taped my Treasure Map on the bathroom mirror so I can see it every day. If I want to journal every night before bed, I'll keep my journal on my pillow. If my goal is to paddleboard twice a week, I'll get out my board and wetsuit the night before so it stares at me in the morning while I make my coffee and reminds me that I wanted to do this. If I want to make pad thai tonight, I'll set those noodles and pans out on the counter before I leave for work. Then when I get home, they'll be there waiting for me, and am I *really* going to put everything away and order pizza again? Probably not.

Alarms and notifications—or the lack thereof—can also be powerful nudges. Your calendar app can remind you of activities you don't want to forget about. Your fitness tracker or smart watch can remind you to take a break and walk around or do some stress-reducing breathing exercises. If you want to stay focused for a while, you can turn off notifications to eliminate distractions.

Your furniture, your clothes, even where you choose to live—all these things can make it either easier or harder to engage in the things you want to do. Convenience always trumps perfection.

For example, if you want to exercise more and are choosing between the gym that's on the way home and the nicer one that's out of the way, pick the convenient one. Then, make sure you have enough workout clothes you genuinely like to wear and feel good in. Set notifications to remind you to go so you don't lose track of time and miss your window. Pack your gym bag every night and put it by the door so you don't forget it. When I plan on working out in the morning, I lay out my workout clothes the evening before so I see them and put them on right when I wake up. I've only been awake for five minutes, but I'm halfway there already.

All these little nudges add up to big changes in behavior. So, look at the things you want to do and ask yourself: What obstacles can get in the way? What inconveniences make it feel hard or unappealing? What conveniences make it too easy to quit? How can you eliminate those?

SELF-IMPOSED CONSEQUENCES

There are always consequences for your choices. The problem is, when it comes to pursuing your personal goals, those consequences are usually a bit too fuzzy and far away. When I was waiting around for business inspiration to strike, I knew I was wasting time, but I didn't know all the things I was missing out on—traveling the world, changing tens of thousands of lives, meeting my future wife.

That's why it helps to create more immediate consequences for yourself. For example, you can hold back something you really want (like watching your favorite show, eating your favorite food, or getting that massage you've been dreaming about) until you've done what you said you would do. You can commit to an actual cash penalty, because sometimes there's nothing more motivating than putting your money where your mouth is. I have a group of four friends that all work out every single morning at seven, and if anyone is late, he has to pay the other three $10 each—and it's $20 each if he's a no-show. Guess how often they are late? Exactly. Leverage fear of loss, which is incredibly powerful, to motivate yourself to act.

Sometimes inconvenience can be your friend too. If you want to start running five miles but have difficulty staying on the treadmill for 30 minutes, instead try for an outside run and go 2.5 miles one way—that way, you have to come home 2.5 miles and there's no cutting it short. Want to take a trip somewhere? Buy a non-refundable ticket so if you bail last minute, you lose your money. Want to learn something new? Pay for a course up-front so if you quit early, you feel it in your pocketbook. If it's too convenient to stop what you're doing, make it less convenient by adding a consequence.

ACCOUNTABILITY PARTNERS

There may be nothing more powerful in achieving our personal goals than an accountability partner, someone who knows what your dreams are and will hold you to them. Social pressure is incredibly compelling—we hate to disappoint others or backpedal on public commitments. And humans naturally thrive on encouragement from others, which is a powerful positive motivator. You can use those natural tendencies to your advantage.

Just having an accountability partner boosts your likelihood of following through to 65 percent.[24] Most astounding of all, having a specific follow-up appointment with that person takes that up to 95 percent. If you had a 95 percent chance of winning the lottery, would you play? Hell yes you would.

So, what exactly does an accountability partnership look like? Sometimes, it's a one-on-one relationship with someone who also wants to achieve the same thing, or something similar. For example, when I decided I really wanted to try stand-up comedy, I found a friend who had the same goal, and we planned our first open mic night together.

Before we got on stage, our nerves were through the roof. I wasn't sure if I wanted to vomit, run away, or drink three shots of tequila. But we were both there—if he was going to get up and do it, well, so was I. Luckily, we weren't terrible, people laughed at (some of) our jokes, and we had fun. But we might have never found that out if we had each gone at it alone and chickened out at the last minute.

For the next few years, we wound up writing a lot of our new material together, practicing it on each other, and even frequently performing in the same comedy clubs on the same nights—all of which kept us both motivated to continue writing and performing, even when times were tough and things got in the way. A business partner, hiking buddy, fellow food lover, workout partner, whatever the case may be—find someone who shares your goal or passion, and they will help you get there.

A more one-sided mentorship or coaching relationship can also provide strong accountability. For example, a personal trainer is a great accountability partner for any exercise activities you want to do. If you want to learn to meditate, a meditation teacher—or even just a more advanced student—would be a perfect accountability partner. These people have been through the struggle of learning a new skill or habit and can help you persist when you might otherwise give up. Some of these obviously cost money, but hey, guess what? That just piles on more motivation when it's something you're spending your hard-earned dollars on.

If you want *really* powerful motivation, find an accountability partner you look up to. That puts you in a bind, in a good way: Would you rather disappoint that person or get in gear and do what you said you would do? Probably the latter.

You can have different accountability partners for different things. They should be people who are patient and supportive but also disciplined and willing to challenge you.[25]

ACCOUNTABILITY IN GOAL SETTING[26]

- Having an idea or goal:
  10% likely to complete the goal
- Consciously deciding that you will do it:
  25% likely to complete the goal
- Putting it on your calendar:
  40% likely to complete the goal
- Planning how to do it:
  50% likely to complete the goal
- Committing to someone that you will do it:
  65% likely to complete the goal
- Having a specific accountability appointment with someone you've committed to:
  95% likely to complete the goal

The relationship works best if you set up a regular time to connect so you can report your progress, encourage each other, and work through any obstacles together.

To find the right person, speak up about what you want to do and invite like-minded people to connect with you. If you talk about your goals with your friends, family, and coworkers, you just might find someone who shares them or who knows someone else who does. There's an online forum for every interest, so if you don't find someone in your local community, you can almost certainly find a remote accountability partner.

When you combine accountability partners with nudges and self-imposed consequences, you create a powerful system to shape your behavior and fill your life with enriching experiences.

Connect Low and High ROI

Valuable experiences come in all shapes and sizes. Some are easy to access and require little time, effort, or money. These include things like going for a walk in nature, cooking something new, reading for pleasure, going on a date to a new place, taking foreign language lessons, or getting up to watch the sunrise. The barrier to entry is low...but so is the return on your investment (ROI). Low ROI isn't a bad thing, though. These experiences might not blow your mind or change your life, but you can do them frequently, and those small payoffs can add up to major value over time.

High-ROI experiences, on the other hand, require a much bigger investment—but there's a bigger payoff too. That's the thing about experiences: you tend to get out what you put in. The more effort it takes, the more value it's likely to bring to your life. Big things like performing on stage, running a marathon, traveling to your dream destination, or getting married really push you to grow as a person and broaden your perspective. They shake up your routine and refresh your appreciation for the little things you love about your daily life.

Ideally, you want to have experiences across the ROI spectrum. If you only focus on low-ROI experiences, you'll miss out on the big personal growth that high-ROI experiences bring. On the flip side, if you focus only on high-ROI experiences, you'll miss out on the little joys that keep day-to-day life fun and interesting. A great way to reach both ends of the spectrum is to use lower ROI experiences to build up to higher ones.

One of the biggest dreams my wife and I shared was to spend time in Italy and eat our way through that beautiful country. Turns out, we weren't alone. In our *Life Experience Survey*, when we asked what the number one experience people want in their lifetimes was, "a trip to Italy" was one of the top answers. We used low- to high-ROI experiences to prepare and eventually pull off an incredibly rewarding trip while having lots of smaller rewards the entire way leading up to it. (To really get the most out of it, we couldn't just book a ticket to Rome and Google "best pizza in Italy.")

The first step was to put it on our calendar. We picked late September because the weather is usually nice and the summer crowds (and pricing) have gone down. Then, we needed to figure out how to pay for it. Our solution was a new Delta SkyMiles credit card with a great sign-up bonus—the bonus plus the miles we earned for our usual, everyday purchases would be enough for two tickets. Just by committing to the date and planning out how to fund it, our brains started to release those dopamine hits of excitement and anticipation.

Once it was on our calendars, we could start dreaming and do the fun "research"—a.k.a. low-ROI experiences that would help us decide where to go, what to do, and, most importantly, what to eat in Italy. We planned movie nights with classics like *Roman Holiday*, *La Dolce Vita*, and *Under a Tuscan Sun*. Next, we leaned into Italian cooking at home. We made pasta and pizza dough by hand and revived my family recipe for slow-cooked meat sauce (Sunday Sugo or Sunday Gravy for the uninitiated). All these tasty and forgiving recipes were inexpensive, fun to make, and not too time consuming. We may or may not have also enjoyed quite a few delightful sips of Italian wine.

As we progressed, we went on date night dinners to new Italian restaurants and wine tastings, where we asked lots of questions about the menus. We wanted to be able to read menus in Italian, so we started expanding our food vocabularies and learning which foods were from which region. From there, we enhanced our limited Italian conversation skills (*Buongiorno!* wasn't going to get us too far) with 10 minutes a day of basic Italian on the Duolingo app. We got competitive on the app to see who could learn the fastest, checking our progress with each other each night.

Through these low-ROI experiences, the picture of our trip became more vivid. We could see more clearly how to focus on our particular interests and make the most of our time there, which greatly enhanced our eventual trip to food heaven. Everything we learned about those delicious meals we created, the wines we tried, and the advice we received from experts and friends became guidance for our planning.

While food was a driving force for this trip, the more we immersed ourselves in all things Italian, the more we knew our trip wouldn't be complete without seeing places like the Sistine Chapel, Colosseum, and Pantheon with our own eyes, eating Roman-style pizza in centuries-old gathering places like Piazza Navona and Campo de' Fiori, and tossing a coin into Trevi Fountain for luck. First stop? A boutique hotel a few blocks from the Spanish Steps, from where we explored the architectural marvels, wandered the seemingly endless maze of ancient cobblestone paths, and soaked up all the charm and rich cultural history central Rome has to offer.

From there, we hopped on a train to Florence to begin the next part of our trip, because one of the most vague but recommended activities from all of our friends was simply: road trip across Tuscany. When we watched *Roman Holiday*, we loved the iconic Italian car culture that the Fiat 500 represented, so we found a place to rent one on the edge of town, making it easy to escape the city and start our driving adventure.

And, of course, we had mapped out our route based on the foods and wines we most wanted to experience. Out of all the foods we tried at our local neighborhood Italian restaurants, we loved the truffle dishes the most. When we learned that truffles from Tuscany were the most sought after, we researched how we could go truffle hunting and booked it. When we arrived at the 15th-century castle in San Miniato, we were taught all about the history, region, and regulations of truffle hunting before being led out to scour the beautiful tree-covered countryside for these hidden gems. Thanks to our faithful truffle hunting dog, Choco, our mission was a great success. We found some of the biggest truffles of the season! We promptly turned them over to our hosts who prepared an incredibly scrumptious, yet simple meal of homemade pasta with olive oil and truffle sauce. *Mamma mia*. This turned out to be one of the best experiences of our trip. *Buon appetito* indeed!

Through our wine tastings back home, we discovered our favorite wines were Chianti and other Sangiovese-based wines like Brunello Di Montalcino and Vino Nobile di Montepulciano. We also discovered those were among the most expensive in the US, but are much cheaper at the source. So, we booked one night each in Montalcino and Montepulciano—and brought home as many bottles as we could to keep reliving the experience.

Can you see how our low-ROI "research" gave us clear direction? Once we figured out Tuscany was where we wanted to spend most of our time, but a shorter stop in

Rome was definitely in order, the rest was just taking steps to make our dream come true. Booking flights, rooms, car, dinner/activity reservations, etc.

When we asked all those pasta lovers in our survey why they hadn't taken their dream trip to Italy yet, many said they simply "didn't know where to start." That's exactly where low-ROI experiences come in. They help you narrow down your vision so the planning process becomes less overwhelming. Anybody can follow the same steps we used. It might take you four months or two years, but if you start with the small, easy experiences now, you'll build clarity and excitement around the big trip—and have fun while you're at it. You'll also keep the dream alive and stay motivated to save your vacation days and extra dollars.

Plus, low-ROI experiences allow you to "test" your dream in a low-stakes way before you commit a lot of resources to it. I mean, what if it turned out you didn't like Italian food and wine as much as you thought? (Ha, yeah right.) It's better to find that out before you invest in plane tickets, take time off work, and build up the experience in your mind.

Most importantly, low-ROI experiences make the big event even more rewarding when it finally happens. All that effort and anticipation amplifies the meaning and power of the experience. You'll be more invested in it, more excited about it, and more prepared to savor every moment because you know what it took to make the experience happen.

Inaction Has Consequences

When I think back to those empty months after I left the shipping company, I often wonder what would have happened if I hadn't acted when I did. Would the people I helped that year have received help from someone else? Would I have ever experienced any of those incredible things? Would Bridget and I have met and started LSTN, helping over 50,000 people get hearing aids? Would I have met my wife? Would I have ever gone to Italy? Would I be writing this book?

Probably not, which is a sobering thought. The amount of positive change that flowed from that moment is staggering, and to think that it almost never happened...it's like I dodged a bullet. If I had waited, it probably would have stayed on my "someday" list, and then just never happened.

The sooner you take action, the sooner you can start your own positive chain reaction. Every day you wait is one day less that you get to enjoy new things, grow as a person, and impact the world. Inaction is a disservice to yourself and all the people you touch.

There is no dream that can't be broken down into small actions. In fact, that's the only way anything big gets done. If you don't start taking those small steps now, the big dream will never materialize, and you'll be just another victim of Someday Syndrome.

The point of this chapter isn't to create a perfect life, with a perfect calendar that you always stick to and perfect habits that you never break. It's to make progress. To take real, concrete steps toward the experiences you want. To weed out, bit by bit, the internal bullshit that gets in your way. To start stacking up that experiential wealth, one day at a time. Some experiences are like mountains in the distance—massive, almost unreal goals that are years away. The only way to get there is one step at a time, and the sooner you start, the sooner you'll arrive.

✦ ✦ ✦

EXERCISES

Low to High ROI

Choose one high-ROI experience from your Treasure Map—something that requires a significant investment of time, effort, and/or money. Then, follow these steps to maximize your likelihood of following through on this dream.

1. Break this experience down into small, achievable steps—the smaller, the better. Make sure each step is a concrete action you can take.

2. Put all the steps on your calendar. If you're not sure how long they'll take or when you'll be able to do them, make your best guess. You can always move them later if needed.

3. Look at the first step. How can you make it as easy and convenient as possible to do it? What consequences will you impose on yourself if you don't do it on time?

4. Brainstorm at least one possible accountability partner for this high-ROI experience, someone who can keep you focused on making progress toward your goal. Draft a message to propose the accountability partnership.

5. Brainstorm at least five low-ROI experiences that could support your high-ROI goal. Put at least one of them on your calendar in the next two weeks.

Note: Go to ExperientialBillionaire.com *to download or print an extended version of this exercise in addition to free experience guides.*

Chapter Six

TURN NEGATIVES INTO POSITIVES

“You cannot stop the waves but you can learn to surf.”

—Jon Kabat-Zinn

Bridget:

One of the first things I discovered when I began to surf was how arbitrary and punishing the ocean can be. You get up on the board, start to feel confident, and before you know it, you're underwater in the wash cycle, the sea tossing you around. Once your flailing is over, you make sure all your limbs are still bending the right way and you take deep breaths, grateful for all that beautiful oxygen in your lungs.

That's not so different from real life. Sometimes a huge wave seems to come out of nowhere and knocks you down, leaving you disoriented and gasping for breath. That's exactly what happened to me in the first months of 2020. I found myself sobbing on my apartment floor for months straight, wondering how everything had changed so quickly, and desperately trying to find a safe and stable shore where I could plant my feet.

It began with the breakup of a five-year relationship. We'd built a life together in San Francisco. He had kids, we had pets, and our social activities revolved around our life as a couple. That all evaporated in an instant when we separated and I moved back to Los Angeles.

The move happened right before the COVID-19 pandemic shutdowns began. People were panicking. People were dying. People were wearing rubber gloves to get mail from their mailbox and spraying down their vegetables with rubbing alcohol. Some people were wearing hazmat suits to the bank, and some were still coughing on me in the elevator. Suffering, both physical and mental, was everywhere. Not to mention, it was confusing as fuck.

Everything hit me like a full-on tsunami. After my separation, I badly needed to get out and have social distractions, and that was simply impossible. On top of that, the pandemic cut LSTN's business in half—along with our salaries. We had to lay off employees who had worked for us for years and felt like family. Our philanthropic partner had to suspend operations. Joe was stuck in the Middle East—he and his wife had taken their newborn baby to visit his in-laws just before the lockdowns began. The neighborhood I had moved to turned into a crime hotbed nearly overnight after so many people lost their jobs. My new place got robbed several times...after I had just lost my job security and spent a small fortune replacing all my stuff.

Every single important anchor in my life had been uprooted: my most personal relationship, the city I lived in, my ability to travel, social activities with friends, my purpose, my safety, and my finances. All of them were disintegrating at once, and my mental and physical health crumbled right along with them.

I was such a mess that I lost 20 pounds because I could barely force myself to eat (and I usually love food more than life itself). I couldn't sleep. I didn't want to do anything. The only thing to look forward to was the end of the day, when I could crawl back into bed, if I even got out of it.

One day, I was morosely unpacking boxes in my new place in LA when I stumbled across a very special matcha teacup. A few years earlier, on a trip to Japan, I had spent a day learning about samurai culture. At the end of my samurai experience, we had a traditional tea ceremony, and as I held my beautiful ceramic cup, I noticed it was filled with uneven gold lines.

When I asked about this interesting detail, the trainer explained Kintsugi, a Japanese philosophy that treats breakage and repair as part of the history of an object, rather than something to disguise. One manifestation of Kintsugi is expressed by a longstanding tradition with broken ceramics. Instead of disposing of the item or fixing it to make it look like new, the cracks are filled with a gold-colored metal. This emphasizes the break instead of hiding it.

As the samurai trainer explained all this, I felt an instant affinity with this philosophy. It's a tangible demonstration of the idea that mistakes, brokenness, and the storms of life can have beautiful effects and shouldn't be hidden or thrown away. Instead, they should be recognized and displayed. It was a powerful reminder that everything—the good, the bad, and the ugly—can serve us, and we should waste no experience.

In that miserable moment, a teacup didn't magically make everything better, but it reminded me that my negative experiences could become a priceless part of my life story. By being destroyed, I realized it was the best time to transform my future. In fact, despite all the fun, thrill-seeking, globe-trotting experiences I've had, the journey to overcome my depression and conquer my mental health is what I consider the most valuable experience of my life.

The Hero's Journey

What has been the most valuable experience of *your* life?

When we asked that in our research survey, one-third of the participants described a negative event—something that caused pain at the time. Here are some examples:

> "My most valuable experience has been being homeless. It taught me no matter what, never give up and keep going even if all odds are against you." —Andre, Philadelphia

> "When my mom got cancer, I realized how fragile life is, and it changed my relationship with her and my perspective on time going forward." —Robert, Las Vegas

> "Being addicted to drugs gave me empathy for other people, and I now work to rehabilitate people who are going through the same problems as I had." —Julia, Juneau

> "I consider my divorce my most valuable experience. Without it I would have lived not knowing my true self for the rest of my life. But I was forced to be alone and figure it all out, and now I'm in a much better place." —Brene, Studio City

> "Getting laid off from a career I thought was the 'right' path was the best experience—it made me look at my life and realize that I only got into that profession because

my parents wanted me to, and now I'm much happier at my new job." —Beau, Henderson

When we think about the value of life experiences, there's a tendency to focus on the positive. The vacation, the great date, the amazing meal, the time you won a trophy (well, it was just for participation, but still). But chances are, the most powerful stories you have to tell are actually about something very serious, maybe even quite harrowing.

It makes sense—when was the last time you saw a great movie or read a fantastic book where nothing bad happened? Never, of course. Where's the meaning in that, let alone the magnetic attraction that keeps you glued to the story?

How about this story: "I woke up today and everything was great! I was well rested, ate a nice breakfast, and had a perfect day where absolutely nothing challenging happened. In fact, everything I wished for came true!"

Yawn. That sounds like an amazing day, but the story sucks. It's totally uninteresting. Nobody cares about the good things in a story unless some bad things get in the way of them. Would you be grateful for the good things in life if there were never bad moments?

Not that the point of your life is to make it a good story, but, well…it kind of is. Because in great stories, relatable characters face big challenges and grow as a result. This is the hero's journey that drives all great stories: a flawed main character goes through a crisis, overcomes obstacles to reach an important goal, and comes out the other side having changed for the better in some way.[27] Now, that's not to say that the only way to grow is through devastating pain (I don't wish that for you), but it is true that tough times force us to take big strides toward becoming our best selves.

The inescapable reality is that life just doesn't always go as planned. High expectations meet disappointment. Relationships turn sour. Accidents, illnesses, and natural disasters happen. Business deals go bad. Just ask any elderly person if they've always had it easy—we guarantee you'll get an earful.

But in the long run, negative experiences often turn out to not be all bad after all, as one of my favorite parables illustrates beautifully.

> When an old farmer's stallion won a prize at a show, his neighbor called to congratulate him, but the old farmer said, "Who knows what is good and what is bad?"
>
> The next day, thieves came and stole the valuable animal. When the neighbor came to commiserate with him, the old man replied, "Who knows what is good and what is bad?"
>
> A few days later, the spirited stallion escaped from the thieves and joined a herd of wild mares, leading them back to the farm. The neighbor called to share the farmer's joy, but the farmer responded, "Who knows what is good and what is bad?"
>
> The following day, while trying to break in one of the mares, the farmer's son got thrown and fractured his leg.

The neighbor called to share the farmer's sorrow, but the old man's attitude remained the same.

The following week, the army passed by, drafting soldiers for the war, but they did not take the farmer's son because he couldn't walk. And the neighbor thought to himself, *Who knows what is good and what is bad?*

And yet, we spend an awful lot of time and energy avoiding the "bad"—anything we expect to be uncomfortable.

As a society, we're kind of obsessed with comfort. We sit on our couch and have Postmates deliver tacos to us, watch a show on Hulu while scrolling through Instagram, and then make the big move from the couch to the bed for the rest of the night. We hate to leave our comfort zones, physically and psychologically. We think of discomfort as an undesirable experience and fantasize about a life where everything we want comes to us effortlessly.

The problem is, there's so much value and growth that exists outside your comfort zone. To stay inside it is to limit your life—not just what you can do but also who you can be and the impact you can have on the world. I'm not suggesting that you actively seek out pain, but if you spend your life avoiding discomfort, you'll miss out on a life of building real wealth.

Let's just consider physical discomfort for a moment. You don't have to be a rugged explorer to enjoy your life, but the truth is, some of the most amazing experiences are strenuous. The most interesting and spectacular places in the world are typically not that easy to access. Getting there often involves long flights, bumpy roads, tough hikes, or nauseating boat rides. You have to pay the price to have priceless memories.

When my friends and I drove around the perimeter of Iceland searching for the northern lights, it took eight days adventuring through freezing, windy, and, at times, sketchy terrain. But when we eventually found them, I cried of joy and screamed at the top of my lungs, marveling at the wonder of our planet as I watched the vibrant colors dance across the sky. I had never seen anything more magnificent in my entire life. That night is forever engraved in my memory, and I never remember or care about any of the discomfort leading up to it. In fact, I'd take that trip again and again rather than sit in a comfortable luxury resort somewhere warm.

Can you live without seeing the northern lights? Sure. You can also live without climbing mountains, swimming in coral reefs, crawling through caves, flying through the air, and sleeping under the stars. You can live without pushing your body to its limits. You can spend your whole life on cushy furniture in climate-controlled rooms if you want... but you'd be missing so much of the world's inner and outer beauty if you did.

Emotional discomfort and psychological discomfort work the same way. Avoiding them means missing out on the positive things that go with them, like the sense of accomplishment after overcoming a frustrating obstacle, or the love before the heartbreak. That's why I like to say my spirit animal is a hermit crab. Hermit crabs demonstrate a willingness to let go of their old shells and be in a vulnerable state while they search for new, bigger shells to grow into. Similarly, humans can benefit from being open to change and being willing to let go of old habits, beliefs, or circumstances that no longer serve them. Embracing change, struggle, and vulnerability can lead to personal growth, new experiences, and a more fulfilling life.

Hermit crab or human, comfort zones can be a dangerous place to live. Think about a commitment (relationship, lease, job, etc.) when you chose comfort over true fulfillment. How might you improve your life by taking risks and embracing things that aren't always comfortable?

Experiences Drive You Forward

In the depths of my depression, the last thing I was thinking about was how these events would change my life in a positive way. When you're going through a terrible time, the most annoying thing in the entire world is when people tell you, "You'll be okay! Just be happy! Time heals all wounds!" Not helpful.

You know what *is* helpful? Doing things—i.e., having experiences.

That's what finally pulled me out of the abyss. I had fallen to a point that was so low, I was genuinely afraid of what might become of me. That's when I decided there was nothing to lose—if I was ever going to be happy again, I had to do something different.

I started small. Every time I wanted to climb back into bed, I chose a healthier activity instead. I walked through parks. I read. I rode my bike. I cooked. Even basic things like taking a bath and cleaning my place helped. None of these things were revolutionary, but they interrupted my established pattern of sitting around passively and wallowing in my pain.

That interruption is powerful because behavior feeds emotions. It's all a big cycle, where emotions influence thoughts, thoughts influence behavior, behavior influences the experiences you have, and your experiences influence your emotions. This cycle is often self-reinforcing. Research shows that about 90 percent of our 60,000 daily thoughts are recycled.[28] We fall into patterns, and those patterns can keep our biology, neurocircuitry, neurochemistry, neurohormones, and even genetic expression stuck in a bad place.

These little experiences started to nudge my emotions in a new direction, and the difference became obvious when I started doing them consistently. One new daily routine drastically changed my mood: doing a simple gratitude practice while watching the sun rise and set each day. It forced me to get up, take my dog outside, and bookend my days by thinking about the positive aspects remaining in my life. It also helped regulate my sleep, which made me feel physically healthier and more energetic. This practice became my favorite part of my day, and I still do it.

It was important that these experiences were small because I didn't have the drive for anything more. But when I took a walk instead of lying down and diving into a downward spiral of depressing thoughts, I felt a little better—at least I could pat myself on the back for getting out of the house. Bit by bit, I started to rebuild the energy and desire for bigger things.

The pain was inevitable, but suffering was optional. As I refocused my mind away from the suffering, novel experiences became more powerful. I tried adrenaline-filled activities like spearfishing and rollerblading down the boardwalk, as well as calming ones like painting, writing poetry, and roasting my own coffee beans. I recreated dishes from places I had visited, working my way from easier ones (like the egg sandwich from Lawson's convenience store in Tokyo and the chai tea from Dishoom in London) to harder ones (bean-to-bar chocolate and home-cured charcuterie).

As restrictions started to loosen a little, I was overjoyed to find my pod of friends interested in doing all sorts of new activities—tie-dying clothes, teaching ourselves to roll sushi, hosting Connect Four tournaments, fermenting and labeling our own hot sauce and pickles, and sneaking out to Venice Beach at midnight to swim in the bioluminescent waves. As bad as the pandemic was in many ways, seeing others try new things with people they love was a bright spot, a small glimpse of what life should be like.

These experiences gave me natural bursts of serotonin and dopamine—feel-good hormones—that jolted me out of my depression temporarily. The novelty forced me to pay close attention to the task at hand, leaving little room to dwell on the past or worry about the future. And when I succeeded at something new, it helped build my confidence and courage.

My personal experience aligns perfectly with scientific research.[29] The evidence states that simply being more present by doing something new stimulates and activates regions of our brain that improve our mood. So, the next time you're feeling life close in on you, put down the remote and try something you've never done before. It's not as easy, but it works.

Grow Through the Pain

It wasn't all about taking my mind off my negative experiences, though. I had to actually learn from them before they could become a valuable part of my life story.

So, it was time to deconstruct myself, my thoughts, and my past actions. I made a commitment to get to the other side of this pain by changing my negative thoughts into positive ones. I knew that happiness was an inside job, and I was the only one who could change how my story ended.

I got a therapist—something I had never even considered before—and was completely vulnerable for the first time in my life. Before, I had refused to seek therapy, to admit I had these patterns and problems, because I didn't think I was as worthy of help as the people I had met throughout the developing world. I thought it was a ridiculous privilege to focus on your own mental health as an American. Obviously, I couldn't have been more wrong, and "comparing" trauma is a losing game. Over time, not dealing with my own issues had caused my relationships with other people and myself to implode, which is what led to this whole situation.

So, I took the time and space to look my demons in the eyes. I dissected patterns from my past, saw the truth about my actions, and took responsibility for their consequences. I thought long and hard about what I could and could not control. I couldn't change the relationship that had ended, but I could control how I handled situations in the future to try to avoid that same pattern.

After the break-ins and breakup, I needed a place to bleed out away from the unsafe, uncertain concrete jungle I was living in. I couldn't control the stress-inducing crime wave in my neighborhood, but I *could* choose to move to a place that felt more tranquil. I had always said that "'someday"' I wanted to move closer to nature, and at this point, I had nothing to lose by trying. I found a place north of Los Angeles by the ocean, smaller but similarly priced, and it drastically improved my mood, my health, and ultimately my lifestyle. Moving was exhausting, but it was absolutely worth the effort to live in a place surrounded by water, trees, sunshine, rocks, and animals—a place that would support my healing instead of undermining it.

I went to the local transcendental meditation center to learn to calm my mind. I started accumulating a bookshelf of knowledge about attachment styles, love languages, Gottman, CBT, enneagrams—modalities I was previously unaware of that helped me understand myself. I wrote down everything I was sorry for and everything I regretted, apologizing to people I knew I had hurt.

A year and a half into my healing journey, I went to an intensive, introspective week-long therapy retreat in Petaluma, California, called the Hoffman Institute. That experience had the single biggest life-altering impact on understanding myself I could have imagined. Never in my life had I bawled from grief and sorrow one day and childlike joy the very next. On the seven-hour drive home down the typically mind-numbing Interstate 5, highlighted by cows and thirsty looking crops, it was like my world had suddenly gone from black and white to technicolor. I felt deeply, authentically alive and free when I realized I had finally gotten to the other side of this massive stumbling block in my life.

For me, as for most people, putting up a mirror to all my problems was extremely uncomfortable. It would have been much easier in the short term to just ignore them, numb myself, and repeat all my same patterns from the past instead of working through them. After all, I had been doing that my whole life. But this time, I chose to use my suffering as an opportunity to learn and grow, and that made all the difference. Instead of just being a black mark on the story of my life, I now look back on that period as a crucial turning point that made me a healthier, happier person and set the stage for a brighter future.

Take Withdrawals From Your Memory Bank

Memories are returns on your investment in experiences. They let you look back on good moments, which can shift your state of mind in powerful ways.

At my lowest point, I went through my photos on my phone and made a folder of my happiest memories. I found a website to print them for cheap and put them up on a small wall in my apartment. The nostalgia helped shield me from wallowing in my pain. Whenever I started feeling blah, the photos made me smile.

Nostalgia is a complex emotion that involves happy memories and a longing for the past, often triggered by sensory stimuli like smells or music. It's a common experience that almost everyone has, and its object tends to change throughout life. While nostalgia was originally considered a disease back in the 1700s (crazy!), research shows it's actually a defense mechanism against unhappiness.[30,31] By recalling positive memories, nostalgia can strengthen social bonds, improve mood, and increase optimism. In fact, studies have found that inducing nostalgia can even lower existential anxiety and increase spirituality.

Photos and small souvenirs (like my teacup) allow us to powerfully relive moments, especially in times when you need to cultivate gratitude. This is our physical bank of memories. But often they get stuck in our phones, computers, or storage never to be seen again. Making the effort to organize these memories and display them where you live is worth doing. Save the memory, and one day, the memory may save you.

One of the most powerful ways I moved through this difficult time is by making a list of the worst experiences I had gone through. For me, these memories served as a reminder that even though I had been through hard times before, I had persevered and was able to have good times afterward. It helped me see light at the end of the tunnel. I thought about the time I had been laid off, but then ended up moving to California for a new job. I remembered the time a huge business deal fell through, which ended up being a blessing in disguise that saved our company. Some of my most awful experiences had turned into valuable lessons or transformed my future. And some of them just became funny stories afterward.

Like the time I went to jail.

You've already heard the story of how I lied my way into an unpaid internship at a record label and then scraped and clawed my way to the coveted mailroom job at $20,000 a year. You know how elated I was when I found out that not only was my foot solidly in the door of the music industry, but I would actually get a real salary and be able to stop couch surfing and stealing company toilet paper.

Not so fast. Less than two weeks later, before I even received my first massive paycheck, as I was stopped at the light at the company parking lot entrance, I heard a sound behind me that every human struggling to pay their bills has had nightmares about: *woop woop*. Blue and red flights flashed. My barely running car got pulled over, right in front of the giant conference room windows of my office building...on a Tuesday at 9 a.m., which just happened to be the exact time of the weekly all-staff meeting.

Everyone in the office got a front row seat to see me pushed up against a cop car, handcuffed, thrown in the back of a cruiser, and hauled off to jail. Several months back, I had received a citation for underage drinking, and it came with a fine I had no intention or ability to pay. When you're so broke you're taking toilet paper from the office, paying fines is very low on the priority list. And since I didn't have a residence, I didn't have a mailbox to receive any court summons.

The government had a different view of the matter. Because of my failure to pay the citation, a warrant was issued for my arrest, and my driver's license had been suspended. I also had expired tags, which is why the police pulled me over in the first place.

My heart sank further and further as I paced back and forth in the cold cell of the local jail. I prayed to every God I could think of that my boss wouldn't see me as the irresponsible delinquent I was and would let me keep my dream job. I felt like my whole future was on the line.

I had no cash for bail, so I was stuck. Using my one phone call from jail, I called my boss to tell him I wouldn't be at work that day. No answer. The voicemail started with a pre-recorded clip—"This is a call from the Detroit jail"—before saying I wouldn't be coming in. Classy!

And then, I just sat on the jail cell bench all day, and then all night, while trying to block out the intimate details of my cellmate Rhonda's story about how she lost two fingers. She also didn't have any ideas on how the hell I was going to get out, save my dream job, get my towed car back, and not see everything I had worked for and fantasized about go up in flames.

I knew my derelict friends didn't have any money, and I would never dare tell my parents (although they're finding out right...now), so I came up with a brilliant plan—humiliate myself further by asking my new boss to bail me out so I could come to work the next day. He already knew where I was, so why not? I desperately convinced him with the reasoning that he knew I would pay him back because he could keep my first few paychecks.

Despite my nearly having a stress-induced heart attack in jail, everything went on as usual. To my surprise, my coworkers didn't think I was unfit to be employed. They just considered the whole thing a hilarious incident about the 19-year-old mailroom clerk who livened up an otherwise boring staff meeting. Being the butt of a joke was a small price to pay for being able to keep my job. Thank God it was far from the worst thing to ever happen in the music industry. Now that I'm older, it's funny to me in the same way it was to them. And now that I'm the boss, I promise to bail out any future employees to pay it forward.

This Too Shall Pass

Nobody aims to have miserable experiences, but we all have them anyway. They are an essential part of what makes life rich.

Sometimes what seems like the end of the world turns out to be the best thing that could have happened to you.

Or just a day and night in jail.

✦ ✦ ✦

EXERCISES

The Only Way Out Is Through

NEGATIVE EXPERIENCES TO POSITIVE MEMORIES

It's tempting to think life would be better if it always ran smoothly, one fun and fulfilling experience after another. We know in our hearts the truth about life is that suffering and hard times teach us lessons that can't be learned any other way. The best teachers of life are failure, betrayal, empty pockets, mistakes, heartbreak, rejections, time, and experience. This exercise helps you reframe negative experiences into positive memories—or at least teachable moments.

1. On a sheet of paper, create three columns. In column one, write down a negative experience.

2. Next to that, in column two, write out how you felt about it at the time.

3. In the final column, write out how the experience seems to you now and what came out of it for you—lessons learned, funny stories, or positive experiences gained because of it.

Some experiences aren't going to feel positive, like losing a family member or a pet. For those, instead of writing about a lesson learned or good outcome, write about why you're grateful for the time you had with them and how it made you stronger or wiser.

TAKING CONTROL AND LETTING GO

If you're dealing with a negative experience in your life right now, this exercise will help you take steps to resolve it and learn from it.

1. Focus on one negative situation in your life right now. It could be financial ("I can't travel where I want to go because I don't have money"), physical ("My bad back is keeping me from playing basketball"), familial ("I'm struggling to care for both my children and my elderly parents"), or anything else weighing you down.

2. What factors are contributing to this situation that you *cannot* directly control? For example, you can't control the weather, the economy, or other people's feelings

and choices. Write them down. Focus on that list for a moment. For each item, take a moment to close your eyes, breathe deeply, and commit to not worrying about it. Worrying about things you can't control only hurts you—it creates unnecessary stress and distracts you from the things you *can* control. Let this stuff go.

3. Now, what are the factors you *can* control? What can you personally do to change the situation, or take yourself out of it? Which of those things can you do today, or better yet, right now? Go do it, or at the very least, put it on your calendar.

Note: Go to ExperientialBillionaire.com *to download or print an extended version of this exercise in addition to free experience guides.*

PART III

Build Wealth

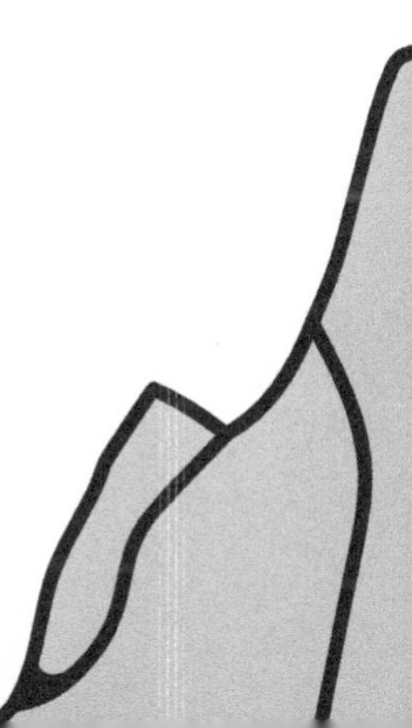

Chapter Seven

PROSPER THROUGH CONNECTION

"The best thing to hold onto in life is each other."

—Audrey Hepburn

Joe:

"How would you like to give away a million dollars?"

As I held the phone, I remember thinking there must be a catch. Mainly because, well, I didn't have anywhere close to a million dollars. But I kept listening because over the last year, the people on the other line had grown from business associates into close friends.

They quickly explained the details of their offer. If I was open to it, I would be one of four judges for that year's Chivas Venture, a contest to provide no-strings-attached funding to socially conscious businesses from around the world—and, of course, they were providing the million dollars I would get to give away. Without a second thought, I said, "Hell, yes!" and asked who the other three judges would be.

They casually listed them off: Alexandre Ricard, the CEO and namesake heir of Pernod Ricard, the 10-billion-dollar parent company of Chivas Regal; Sonal Shah, founding executive director of the Beeck Center for Social Impact and Innovation at Georgetown University and the Director of Social Innovation for The White House; and Eva Longoria, A-list actress and activist who needs no further introduction.

Wow. I was stunned. To be even considered alongside the other three judges was an honor. My self-declared title of "Director of Positivity" at LSTN paled in comparison to their extraordinary accomplishments. So, I asked the obvious next question of, "Why me?" They told me my experience working with social enterprises over the last decade gave me unique insight that would prove valuable. But I knew many entrepreneurs had those credentials—and many worked for much larger and better-known organizations.

So, how and why was I the one being offered this amazing experience? I believe it came down to one thing: relationships.

Over the course of the previous year, we had turned a conversation about promotional products into a full blown brand collaboration between LSTN and Chivas to raise funding and awareness for our charity partner. Together, we sold millions of limited edition promotional whisky tins at luxury retailers, airport duty free shops, and Costco; crafted bespoke, high-end record consoles from the staves from whisky barrels; and produced a custom Spotify "listening" campaign. Each sale and stream directly resulted in a donation to Starkey Hearing Foundation. To drive awareness for the campaign, we cohosted events in Beverly Hills and London that featured our own custom cocktail, the "Honey Rider," inspired by Bridget's love of whisky and ginger and my passion for tequila. Not sure how having a custom drink named after us hadn't made it onto any of our "life goals" lists before that.

To create marketing assets for the collaboration, we spent a week in Scotland with the Chivas team. We all stayed together in The Linn House, a haunted 19th century Scottish Baronial Mansion sitting on the banks of the River Isla, where Bridget and I "modeled" for their huge print and billboard campaign (for future whisky modeling, call my agent, please). But they didn't just take photos—they gave us an immersive experience of their world.

We learned the craft of making whisky with the master distiller at Strathisla distillery, the oldest continuously operating distillery in the Scottish Highlands. Traditional coopers showed us how they make and repair the wooden barrels used to age Scottish whisky in much the same way they have for hundreds of years. We suited up in safety gear and worked alongside these master craftsmen, where they taught us how to use time-honored tools like mallets and wedges and how to roll the restructured casks over to the massive fiery infernos used to char them. We enjoyed drams of whisky drawn straight from the decades old casks in the dank, musty, centuries-old cellar. We dressed up in traditional Scottish kilts and were serenaded by bagpipes. We ate haggis, the savory pudding containing sheep's pluck (heart, liver, and lungs) minced with onion, oatmeal, suet, and spices—encased in the animal's stomach. Yum. It was presented to us with a traditional song (and much theatrical flair)—appropriately called "Address to a Haggis"—which had us all laughing at lyrics such as "great chieftain o' the puddin'-race." I'll never think of haggis the same again.

In the end, the campaign was a huge success. We used the proceeds to sponsor a philanthropic hearing mission to the Dominican Republic, where it was our turn to bring the Chivas team into our world. We spent a week on the ground in Santo Domingo and Santiago, standing side by side as we helped thousands of people receive the gift of hearing. We watched in awe as a five-year-old boy named Royneld, who was born with little to no hearing, started communicating as he never had before within minutes of receiving his new hearing aids. We cried together with 11-year-old Estefani, becoming overwhelmed with emotion when she regained her hearing after losing it when she was just a toddler. The last morning we were there, we woke up to our pictures on the front page of the local newspaper, fitting a smiling boy with hearing aids, and with huge smiles on all of our faces as well.

It was a fitting ending to a year filled with intense, meaningful shared experiences. We built camaraderie, trust, and deep respect for each other, far beyond the level of a typical business relationship. So, when it came time to pick the fourth judge for the Venture contest, they called on me instead of some other, more famous entrepreneur.

It reminds me of a famous African proverb from Burkina Faso that says, "If you want to go fast, go alone. If you want to go far, go together."

I've known this to be true for a long time.

When I turned my life around in high school, it was with the help of close friends and family who had known me my entire young life. They believed in me when I said I really wanted to clean up my act and go back to school, and they gave me the support I needed. To this day, I'm certain I would not have pulled it off without them.

When I started the apparel shipping company, it was with a close childhood friend, one of the only people I stayed in touch with after high school. We had shared countless deep, meaningful experiences together, both good and bad. We both overcame rough starts, moved away from everyone we knew, and had worked hard to try and make something of ourselves. No matter how infrequently we spoke or saw each other, we showed up for each other when we needed it most—like the time I dropped everything to help care for him and his family while he recovered from a stroke at age 30. As a result, we trusted each other with our lives. Without that bond, I highly doubt he would have trusted me with his very finite savings, which we used to start the business.

When my dad passed away and I felt the calling to do something else, I got direction and support from my friends in the business community I had become a part of. Those were relationships I had built over a decade of attending trade shows and events, and although we didn't see each other often, our wild adventures far from home had made them feel like family to me. Without their help, things probably would have turned out quite differently—not in a good way.

Even now, as Bridget and I sought help with the creation of this book, we leaned on the shoulders of our friends who had been in this arena before. Their invaluable advice and guidance helped us move things forward years faster than we would have been able to do on our own.

Over and over, other people have lifted me up and taken me further than I ever could have gone alone. And all of those relationships were forged through shared meaningful experiences.

In short, meaningful experiences build strong relationships, and strong relationships lead to more fulfilling experiences.

Building relationships takes effort; we only get out what we put in. But it's worth the investment of time and energy because it's through our relationships that we find meaning, support, success, and satisfaction. In that light, tending to your social life is actually an essential form of self-care. The next section covers how to use experiences to create more joy and connection in your relationships with yourself, your inner circle, your friends, and your colleagues.

Be Your Own Best Friend

It may seem counterintuitive to talk about the importance of your relationship with yourself after I just told you how important tending to your social life is.

That's true, but here's another truth: You are the only person who always has been and always will be with you. As the saying goes, "Wherever you go, there you are." We can't escape ourselves (many have tried, all have failed), and there will inevitably be moments in life when you're alone. If you don't like yourself or enjoy your own company, those moments will be painful.

If your relationship with yourself is fragile, you'll tend to seek validation from others to shore it up, and that constant focus on *receiving* love often gets in the way of *giving* it—which is the key to building healthy, mutually rewarding relationships.

Loving yourself is a critical first step to loving others in a healthy way. But sometimes loving and believing in ourselves is harder than it sounds. We get caught up comparing our behind the scenes to everyone else's highlight reel. It's helpful to be honest about your shortcomings. It's destructive to always be your own worst critic.

The cure is...Get. Over. Yourself.

Because the truth is, most people are not paying attention to us—they're focused on themselves. On the surface, this is depressing. *Wait, no one thinks of me?* But it's actually liberating.

When you think negatively about yourself or your abilities to do something, ask yourself these questions: "Am I being judgmental or overly critical of myself? Would I think this way about a friend? Would I let someone else say that about me?" Probably not.

Stand up for yourself. Be proud of yourself. Love yourself. Because your relationship with yourself is, in many ways, the foundation of all your other relationships.

You wouldn't bring someone you didn't like to a party. Well, life is the party, and you need to love yourself so you can show up and party with the best of them. Bringing the version of yourself you actually like to all of your other relationships will make those relationships better.

So, how do you get closer to yourself? Spend quality time with you. What's the best way to do that? Solo experiences. They help you figure out who you are and who you want to be. They help you discover what you genuinely like and dislike, without being swayed by other people's opinions. And, most importantly, they help you cherish your own company and become your own best friend.

When my wife and kids aren't home, I'll go to the movies, museums, art galleries, and local concerts on my own. I've taken salsa lessons, archery lessons, cooking classes, and played a few games at the local bowling alley. When I was younger, I would have thought it was at best antisocial and at worst just plain weird to do any of this alone, but I got over my worries about what other people think, and guess what? I now love going solo in public.

If you'd rather keep it low-key, there are plenty of more private activities you could try. Find a new bike path. Read a book at a coffee shop. Visit an animal adoption center. Try a new recipe, or just make one up. I have an old Triumph motorcycle, and one of my favorite alone-time activities is just driving around the windy roads of Malibu Canyon on an early Sunday morning, where I can be alone with my thoughts (and channel my inner James Dean).

Even more low-key than that? Well, if you wanted to get to know someone better, you would probably just have a conversation with them, right? But if the person you're trying to get to know better is yourself, people will probably look at you funny if you start having a heart-to-heart chat with yourself. Luckily, that's what journaling is for. There's no better way to learn about yourself than to read (or write!) what's on your mind. You can clear your thoughts and hear your truths with unbiased and uncorrupted filters—and best of all, no judgment. I've been journaling since I was in my twenties and I still learn new things every day. Give it a shot—I bet you'll learn a few things about yourself.

Sometimes, solo is the best way to go. You don't have to wait on someone else, coordinate, compromise, or worry about whether your companions are having a good time. You can just do what you want, how you want, when you want, and enjoy it regardless of what anyone else might think. In those situations, dragging someone else along—especially if they're not as excited about the experience as you are—just makes it worse. I'm not saying you should become a selfish jerk and start neglecting your friends and family and only do things by yourself because it's convenient. Just don't let the lack of a partner in crime stop you from doing things you would enjoy.

For the ultimate get-to-know-yourself adventure, book a solo trip somewhere. It doesn't have to be too far away or too long; just get away by yourself. It's a great way to spend time without anyone who "knows" you influencing what you do with your time.

But don't expect to be guaranteed alone time on that "me" trip. Ironically, even though most people are afraid to travel solo because they think it will be boring or lonely, those trips usually end up quite the opposite. We've all heard magical stories of meeting that special someone or new best friend while on a trip. That's because solo travelers are a magnet for curious strangers. You don't even need to worry about how to start a conversation with someone. Just make yourself accessible—at a bar, in a lobby, on a park bench, anywhere public—and they'll come to you. People want to know what you're doing there and make you feel welcome.

You never know where it might lead; a casual conversation might be just that, or it could lead to an invitation to share an experience, or the start of a new friendship. Sounds cliché, but the old maxim is true: Most strangers are just friends you haven't met yet.

These brand new people might respond to you or appreciate you in ways that are different from what you experience with your friends and family. One trip to Paris really highlighted how different traveling solo is from traveling with family or friends. My wife, Yasmine, and I had planned to spend two months in Paris after we got married, but due to some other commitments, she had to come a few days later than me. So, for four days, I explored the St. Germaine neighborhood where we were staying and assaulted local shops, cafés, restaurants, and bars with my God-awful attempts to speak French.

I always started with an apology: *Je suis désolé mon français est très mauvais.* ("I'm sorry, my French is very bad.") Then, before I could continue to butcher every word in their beautiful language, they would usually interrupt me and say, "It's okay, English is fine."

This generally led to questions, conversations, and helpful suggestions. Sometimes it even led to invitations, one of which resulted in a fun night drinking champagne at some obscure spot in Paris that I am a hundred percent sure I would have never discovered on my own (and after all the champagne, I'm also a hundred percent sure I could never find it again).

When Yasmine showed up four days later, she laughed as we walked through the neighborhood, and the shop owners, bartenders, and waiters all smiled, waved, and said, *Bonjour!* to me. Solo Joe had made friends with a few dozen people and learned all about the neighborhood in just a few days. But, from then on, we had each other for constant companionship and conversation, and we hardly met anyone at all. Even though we were there for two full months, I made far more new connections in those four days alone.

If you're not one to spend much time alone, you don't need to jump straight into a big solo trip far from home. Start small, maybe with something you've been putting off because you didn't have anyone to do it with. Try that new Vietnamese restaurant, take that spin class, or go see that punk rock show. Take a day trip to wine country, or rent a kayak at the lake. Enjoy the place. People watch. Daydream. Be present. Tell everybody you're busy, and turn off your phone. Give yourself some quality time with yourself. You'll have a memorable new experience, and who knows, you might even meet your new best friend or romantic partner.

Nurture Your Inner Circle

In 1938, Harvard University began tracking the physical and mental health of 268 sophomores.[32] They followed up with these students every few years, hoping to learn about what led to a happy and healthy life. Eighty years later, they have a pretty good idea: close relationships.

The study illustrated how warm, close relationships with our best friends and family members were linked to less depression, less incidents of dementia and memory loss, and longer life spans. Read that last part again. Nurturing your inner circle will not only make you happier and healthier but can also make you *live longer.*

Inversely, if you let yourself become isolated and lonely, you're definitely cutting down on your odds of a long, happy life. In a 2015 TED Talk about the Harvard study, Robert Waldinger summed up the data in this powerful way: "Loneliness kills. It's as powerful as smoking or alcoholism." It might sound morbid or depressing, but those stark words are an important reminder of what's at stake.

Your inner circle is for the people closest to you, whether that's your romantic partner, your family, or your best friends who are as good as family. They're the ones you spend the most time with and reveal the most of yourself to. While all your relationships are important, these relationships have the greatest impact on your mental and physical health, in the short run and the long run, so keeping them strong should be a top priority.

The paradox is that, because you spend so much time with these people, it's easy for the relationship to fall into a rut, where everything is the same, day in and day out. Maybe they live with you, or they're around all the time, so you don't have to make plans to see them. Next thing you know, complacency kicks in, and the amount of effort we put in wanes—and as a result, you hardly ever do anything special together.

So, over time, the spark begins to fade. The bonds that were forged over late night bottles of wine and romantic walks in the woods weaken, and the friction of day-to-day conflict sets in.

In the beginning of a close relationship, you're always looking forward to something—the next milestone, the next first time. Those things give you something to focus on, work toward, and get excited about. As soon as there's nothing to look forward to, things go sideways. You get mired in the mess and monotony of daily life, and that's when the wheels fall off.

I get it. When my wife and I became parents, like most people with young kids, our social life slowed *way* down. We took on the classic grown-up roles: work all day, then find time to clean, cook, play with the kids, and do the thousand other things required to keep the gears of life in motion. In our brief windows of free time, sometimes all we wanted to do was catch a few hours of rest—if that was even possible between the endless parade of playdates, soccer practice, and gymnastics classes. Sometimes we felt like we barely had time to breathe, let alone plan novel experiences together.

But we knew that would be taking the easy way out. It's easier to order pizza than make our own from scratch. It's easier to buy the kids a new toy than organize a scavenger hunt for secret "treasure" in the park. It's easier to put them in front of a nature documentary on TV than go to the zoo and see tigers and lions and monkeys in real life. But which of these things create special memories that bring us closer together?

As a family, we've stretched our limits (physically, mentally, and definitely financially) to do special things and go to special places. Locally, we've made magical memories in places like Ojai Valley, Yosemite, Joshua Tree, and Big Sur. Farther afield, we've caught fireflies in New York, swum with manta rays and sharks in Tahiti, fed parakeets in London, and gone reindeer sledding in Norway. To make those things happen wasn't easy. There was backpacking with heavy kids on our shoulders, camping in the freezing desert, long plane rides, sometimes even longer car trips, uncomfortable boat rides in stormy weather, dirty diapers, peed pants, projectile vomiting, and all the other pain points of family travel. And, of course, there was the time and money we spent.

But those experiences and the memories they created are forever—and were worth every bit of effort and then some. What could possibly be more important than that?

According to research, by the time our children are 18 years old, we've spent 93 percent of the time we will share with them in our lives. Make those years count. Our children and families are not obstacles but opportunities, ways of re-constituting what's important, ways of creating urgency, joy, purpose, and perspective.

Many times our best friends are even closer to us than our extended family. After all, we get to choose them. As a result, we usually put a lot more effort into making those relationships work—which can pay off with some of the most incredible experiences.

When I first moved to LA, one of my best friends was struggling to find work and really needed a place to stay. I let him move in and crash on the couch until he got on his feet. Living together bonded us further, as we shared our struggles and spent more time together—so much that we often told people we were cousins to explain why we were always together.

A few years later, his career was skyrocketing and he was prospering. At the same time, I was in a dark place. I was entering the apex of my bankruptcy crisis and dealing with a close friend's suicide. He knew I was struggling, so he invited me on a business trip—to Australia. We flew first class and stayed in a mansion on a private island. I had less than $100 in the bank at the time. I came home with a happy head and a full heart and started to turn my life around.

This is an extreme example, but that's the point. When you show up for your inner circle, they'll show up for you, sometimes with just a couch to sleep on and other times in ways you would hardly have imagined possible. Without those close relationships, I wouldn't have had many of my most valuable experiences. I'm sure when you think about your own life, you can see how your family and best friends have shaped your experiences—and how your experiences shaped those relationships. Those are the people who will go to war with you. When you need help, support, or just a shoulder to cry on, you look to the people you have deep, meaningful connections with.

That's why it's so important to plan novel experiences with your inner circle. They're critical to your collective well-being. They give you something to look forward to. They take you out of the familiar settings where your conflicts live and reset your perspective on the relationship. Hopefully, they remind you why you love each other and give you the chance to reconnect on a deeper level.

So, think about how you can give the people in your inner circle valuable experiences. They don't have to be extravagant or expensive. Make that romantic dinner at home—rose petals, candles and all. Dress up as your kid's favorite superhero or cartoon character and surprise them at the park with a character meet and greet. Throw your best friend a surprise party for no reason other than to celebrate them. For the next holiday or birthday, skip the material gifts and plan a shared experience instead, like a pottery class, whale watching, camping trip, glass blowing, or horseback riding. I always ask for experiences as gifts.

Give as much as you can to those closest to you. Do this without expecting anything in return, because the acts of giving and sharing are extremely rewarding on their own.

But don't be surprised when all your efforts come back in spades, either.

Show Me Your Friends and I'll Show You Your Future

Even if you have a strong family, romantic partner, or best friend, they can't be *everything* to you. You won't always share the same interests or want to do the same things, and there may come a time when the relationship fails altogether. When that day comes, you'll need other people to lean on—your friends.

Your wider social circle of friends is rich in all kinds of other benefits that your closer and more intense relationships don't provide. It can expose you to people with different backgrounds, personalities, and skills, which can stimulate your own growth and creativity. Friend groups are fertile grounds for new ideas and collaborations, as well as job opportunities and business connections.

While you share your deepest and most personal experiences with your inner circle, the broader community you are a part of usually has a greater influence on your general behaviors. Don't underestimate the power of those bigger groups of friends to shape your life, for better or for worse. As the saying goes, "Show me your friends and I'll show you your future."

Surround yourself with communities of people who dream big and take action, and they'll inspire you to do the same. If you want to be creative, hang around other creatives. If you want to be fit, hang out with people who love to exercise. Spend time with people you admire. Because I hate to break it to you, but if you hang around with five friends who are smokers, you'll wind up the sixth.

This is exactly why I moved away from the crowd of people I grew up with. They had all the same bad habits and issues that I had, and I wanted to change. I knew I needed to surround myself with people who had the characteristics, habits, hobbies, and goals I wanted for myself. People who I aspired to be like.

Who did I spend the most time around? Entrepreneurs. What did I become? An entrepreneur.

When you surround yourself with people you admire and who help you grow and try new things, the experiences you share create stronger and more lasting relationships.

That's because when we grow, we experience new things, and the more novel the experience, the closer it brings you. Novelty expands your perception of time, especially in retrospect: looking back, a new experience feels like it lasted longer than it really did.[33] That makes it feel like you've known the people who shared that experience with you for longer, even if you didn't tell your life stories and bare your souls to each other.

When people experience new things together, they view each other as sources of inspiration and personal growth, which further strengthens your bond.

Think about it: When have you felt the tightest bonds form? When have you felt closest to the people around you? When you look back on a relationship, what's on the highlight reel?

That's right: the trips, special events, first times, unusual circumstances, and big challenges. That seven-state road trip, the concert you snuck into, when the tour bus broke down in the middle of nowhere and everyone had to walk, the scavenger hunt, the two-day corporate retreat where it rained so hard everything flooded, the escape room, that three-day activity-filled destination wedding, that wild night of truth or dare. Not day-to-day monotony, but stand-out moments when something new and different was happening.

Those are the times when we get closer and learn to really know and trust each other.

These shared experiences don't have to be complicated, expensive, or wildly creative to be novel. You don't have to go to a faraway place like Scotland, Australia, or France to create these moments and build these bonds. In fact, one of my favorite social experiences was a classic activity that most kids have done before: a sleepover.

It was organized by my friend who lived in Sedona, Arizona. She invited friends from all over the country—almost all of whom didn't know each other—to come for an old-fashioned weekend of hanging out. There were 20 of us, and we all slept outside in sleeping bags on the cramped deck overlooking the majestic red rocks of Sedona. We cooked together, played games, hiked, and just talked. Those might not sound like "novel" activities, but the whole event transported people out of their daily environments and habits. As a result, it forged relationships that will live on for years to come. They may not be in my inner circle, but a decade later, I'm still friends with those 20 people.

Think of it like this. Your inner circle is like a garden that must be diligently tended. The rest of your enduring friendships are more like the forest—big, strong trees that don't need your constant attention. You can leave them alone and come back, and they will still be there: the friends you can call after a year or more has passed and pick up right where you left off. I can tell who those friends are because of the memories or feelings I get when I see or hear their name.

They're the people who have shared some of my most memorable moments in time, even if it wasn't over a long period or if it was just something we did once or twice. We've had the honor of sharing a valuable memory together—and it forever connects us.

But you have to make sure and come back to them. If you don't, you'll find yourself in the situations listed in our global *Life Experience Survey*.

> "When I was in the Army, I had a great group of buddies that I would give anything to see now, but a lot of them are now passed." —Jack, Chattanooga

> "I lost the girl of my dreams because I had to move for a job, and I regret not keeping in touch with her afterwards and now it's too late." —Bronson, Montpelier

> "In college, I was in sorority and one of my biggest regrets is losing touch with those women who were there for me in my formative years." —Sarah, New Haven

> "When I retired, I lost touch with all my coworker friends from my long career in the automotive industry—I wish I still talked to them." —George, Jersey City

When you read those, it makes sense that one of the top five regrets of the dying is, "I wish I stayed in touch with my friends."

Having that forest of strong trees is so valuable, but making friends as an adult in today's world can be hard. Once you've graduated from school, there's no default community to provide you with the casual social interactions that lead to friendships. More people than ever are working from home and don't even have office buddies to turn to. Your old friend groups disperse over time as people move away for jobs and family. Especially if you're in a relationship, it's all too easy to let those friendships disappear and never replace them. That's why it's important to not just maintain, but to keep making friends throughout adulthood.

Asking for direct help is a great way to meet people with the same or similar interests. Go on your favorite social media app and ask for help with a goal. "I really want to learn to rock climb, but I've always been scared to do it. Does anyone know a place I can go for lessons?" Or, "I'd love to organize a burger lover's group to go out and try all the best burger joints in the city. Do you know anyone who would be interested?" People are generally eager to help connect people if they think they can help facilitate a friendship or mutually beneficial relationship.

You can make friends anywhere, if you're willing to put yourself out there and say hello to people. Local organizations, events, gyms, parks, clubs, and sports leagues are all great places to make new friends.[34] Look for opportunities to pursue your favorite hobbies in public or in a group, and you'll find like-minded people there.

For example, my wife is learning how to play the ukulele, and one day she decided to take her ukulele on a walk to the park with the kids so she could strum some chords while they played. Another woman walking by saw her strumming and stopped to tell her that she and some other people in our neighborhood play ukulele together in the park every Saturday morning. Now, I don't know about you, but I *never* would have guessed there was a ukulele club in my own neighborhood. So, get out there, do stuff, and interact with people. You never know.

Regardless of where you find your friends, remember that novel shared experiences are the key to turning acquaintances into forever friends. That's what turns your friends into the strong, tall trees that stick around for years to come, even if you don't always actively tend them.

Work On Your Work Relationships

If you have a full-time job, you spend at least a third of your waking life working. That's a lot of time to be surrounded by your boss, colleagues, clients, and business partners. The stronger those relationships are, the happier and more successful your work life will be—and shared experiences play an important part in that.

A recent Gallup study found that having a best friend at work is closely related to important business outcomes.[35] People who have a best friend at work are more likely to feel satisfied at work, recommend their employer to others, and plan to remain in their job. They contribute to greater profitability, safety, innovation, customer service, and more.

The data shows this, but you already knew it intuitively. Think about your own working relationships. You're most productive when you're in a positive, relaxed mood, which is more likely when you're surrounded by people you like. You collaborate best and resolve conflict faster with people you trust and respect.

When relationships are toxic, the results are disastrous. Communication is totally ineffectual, fraught with misunderstandings and tension. People deliberately undermine each other. They get frustrated with the constant dysfunction and disengage from their work. And, of course, unhappy people don't perform at their best. At the most extreme, poor workplace relationships are enough to topple a company that would otherwise have been successful.

So, it's worth the time and effort to cultivate strong relationships with your coworkers—and if you're a business leader, it pays dividends to foster those relationships. Perhaps this used to be a natural phenomenon, but in today's world, not so much. When so many of us aren't in the same physical space, it takes more deliberate effort.

The key is to intentionally make time for social experiences at work. We can bond more with people through one shared experience than we can from sharing a cubicle with them for five years.

Start a new lunchtime tradition like hosting your own version of Shark Tank. Everyone loves coming up with and hearing new or funny ideas. Make it mandatory that everyone has to genuinely pitch their ideas with as much passion as they can muster. Encourage the use of props like in the show (models, diagrams, stick figures, etc.). This is a guaranteed way to get people to have fun, laugh, and bond—and possibly come up with the next Squatty Potty.

How about sharing new "secret skills" each month where you and your coworkers teach each other your respective hobbies? You fancy yourself a pro at darts? Bring in a dart board and show off your pub skills. Dave in accounting is into martial arts? Everybody goes to his dojo one week and dons a gi while Dave throws high kicks at cinder blocks. Lisa in HR is into black magic? (Of course she is.) Have her host a seance or bring in her Ouija board. The sky's the limit. You'll be surprised what the "hive" knowledge possesses. Throughout, give each other tips and best practices on how to get the most out of the experiences.

Organize an office olympics with outdoor games, teams, and flags. Stage your own version of *The Office*. Get matching tattoos, or just compare the ink you already have and tell the stories behind it.

At the very least, you can do the Treasure Map exercise with your coworkers and set up a Slack channel so everyone can share their goals, root each other on, and help each other achieve them.

If you're the boss, pick a great experience (or have everyone vote on some within the budget) to gift someone every quarter. It can be employee of the month, top salesperson, least accidental deaths, doesn't matter. Just make it a contest the team can get excited for and bond over.

And, of course, if your office is a bit—ahem—"stuffy," you can always go with the good ole "bring your dog or kid to work" day.

These experiences can dramatically change how you and your colleagues view each other. Instead of staying serious and focused, you can joke, laugh, and share things that normally wouldn't come up at work. You'll start to see each other as real people, with histories and families and interests beyond what you see day-to-day at the office. That's how true friendship begins.

Plus, you never know where those relationships may take you. It's not by chance that so many business people play golf; the social experience builds trust and loyalty with other people in their industry. Even if they're not doing a deal today, one day they might. Or they might get a referral, a job, or some other opportunity as a result of those relationships. Three or four hours together on a golf course is long enough to have more personal conversations than months of the five-minute quick hellos and goodbyes you usually have at work.

It doesn't have to be golf, but it's a good example of a great relationship-building activity because it creates plenty of time to talk in an informal, fun environment where everyone is doing something together. There's a shared focus, but it's not too intense or competitive. If you and your colleagues aren't the golfing type, lots of other activities can meet these criteria: pickleball, fantasy sports, karaoke, pranks, cold plunge challenges, the list goes on and on. And if you have a great boss or work at an open-minded company, maybe you can even get them to buy a fun office game like foosball, pinball, or ping pong.

Remember, the activities don't have to be some huge thing, but the more awesome and memorable the things you do with these people are, the deeper and more valuable those bonds will run.

If you were thinking, *I don't have time to socialize at work*, now hopefully you're starting to understand: you don't have time *not* to. The time might not be billable, but the investment will pay dividends in your own satisfaction at work. Whether it's your team, your clients, or your vendors, when you have a personal layer and foundation to those relationships, they become more than transactional. They become people who will root for you, stay with you through the hard times, and sing your praises to others.

You can't wait for perfect circumstances to start living your life, and you can't wait to start nurturing your most important relationships either. Each relationship is a story, and you have to keep adding new chapters to keep the story alive.

The secret to strong bonds lies in shared experiences, especially novel ones. With yourself, your romantic partner, kids, parents, roommates, your ride-or-die, buddies, classmates, colleagues. It doesn't matter. People are people, and experiencing new things brings us together in a powerful way.

✦ ✦ ✦

EXERCISES

Make Your Relationships Prosper

SELF

Have an experience by yourself that you would normally do with someone else. For some people this could be as big as an overseas trip, for others it could be going to the movies, a baseball game, or a class. Take notice of how you feel doing this on your own.

INNER CIRCLE

Have the "best day ever" with your partner, close family member, or best friend. What would your best day ever look like? Write down and plan a list of as many fun activities you can fit into one day as possible. Document and share it to inspire others to do their own "best day ever." For a decade, my email signature ended with "Have the best day ever," which always reminded me and my friends to have more days like this.

FRIENDS

One of the top regrets of the dying is "not keeping in touch with friends." Make a list of people you've lost touch with but still think about. Why do they matter to you? It's probably the ones you've shared some important experience or chapter of your life with. Would you regret it if you never spoke to them again? Pick one and start by reaching out to them today. Don't wait. These are the relationships that matter. This is one regret you can avoid for free with just a phone call, email, or text.

WORK

Who is someone at work or school that you'd like to get to know better? Think about an experience they might like to do and invite them to do it with you. It can be as simple as trying a new lunch spot together, but challenge yourself to be more creative, especially if you already know something about their interests.

Note: Go to ExperientialBillionaire.com *to download or print an extended version of this exercise in addition to free experience guides.*

Chapter Eight

BELIEVE

IN THE MAKE BELIEVE

“Play is the highest form of research.”

—Albert Einstein

Bridget:

Anyone who knows me knows about my chosen vice: natural (aka "natty") wine. I talk about it all the time, to the point of being annoying. I'm in love with the unique and expressive flavors, I obsess over the artwork like it's an album cover, and enjoy reading the stories of small batch makers from all over the world. Sometimes I enjoy it a little too much.

So, I decided it would be fun to learn about the grown-up grape juice process by becoming the world's most amateur home winemaker. I researched how to make it at home and bought the supplies online, which were fairly easy to find: glass jugs, a heating pad meant for plants, thermometer stickers, airlocks, special yeast, and, of course, grapes and sugar.

But I didn't just want to make the wine. I wanted to *celebrate* it, however delicious or atrocious it might turn out to be. I wanted to share the fun with other people, even if they didn't care half as much—or one percent as much—about natural wine as I did.

So, a month later, when the wine was ready to drink, I made a fake brand, simple website, and printed out labels for the bottles. I invited my friends over for a tasting of "Pizza Wine," as I lovingly called my brew. (Someone had once asked me what I would want my last meal to be, and I responded immediately: homemade pizza and natural wine.) But there was a catch. To enter the gathering, each guest had to write and perform a jingle for Pizza Wine.

For example (imagine this sung to the tune of "Surfin' USA" by the Beach Boys):

It's Friday night and we're feeling, oh so fine
Your friend's making pizza, she said you bring the wine
You want something special, that pizza's so cheesy
Our Pizza Wine makes your job, so fuckin' easy

We all sat around my living room watching and giggling like little kids as everyone had their turn.

The prize for winning the competition? More wine. And more pizza.

While the food and drink weren't Michelin starred, and my friends oddly haven't won any Grammys for their monumental achievements in the musical arts, it was the most memorable wine tasting of my life. As my friends and I ugly-laughed to the point of tears, we wondered out loud, "Why don't we do this more often?"

It reminded me of when my sister, my cousins, and I used to do talent shows for each other. We would create our own songs and dances, do magic tricks, juggle, or hula hoop, and giggle for hours.

Why did we ever stop?

Oh, yeah. Because as we got older, it wasn't cool to be silly anymore. We got self-conscious. We thought we should "grow up." And when we did, there was so much serious stuff to do in life that there was no time for that kind of frivolity anymore. Our adult lifestyle, filled with constant busyness, stress, and digital distractions, disconnected us from the joy and therapeutic benefits of play.

I bet the same thing happened to you, too.

But it doesn't need to be that way.

The Science of Play

When did *you* stop playing? And by playing, I mean doing something just for fun, with no goals or expectations about the outcome. Even if it's a game with winners and losers, the result doesn't matter, and your aim isn't to get better over time. It's just to enjoy. (Consuming entertainment doesn't count—real play involves your active engagement, beyond just watching a screen or turning the page.)

As a kid, practically all you wanted to do was play. Every other activity (school, homework, chores, family dinner) was something you had to get through so you could go play.

But little by little, other things became more important. It's not just that you now spend more (or most) of your time making sure bills get paid, people get taken care of, chores get done, etc. There's been a social and psychological shift in priorities, too. Society expects adults to be productive, responsible, and serious; play is a luxury reserved for children. So, you might feel like it's immature to play, and other people would judge you for it. And the less you play, the less exercise your imagination gets, and the more focused you become on practical matters—perpetuating the downward spiral of playtime.

Over time, the things you used to play at become serious endeavors, or to-do list items, or no longer worth doing at all. Running around with your friends outside becomes running on the treadmill at the gym, scheduling coffee dates to see your friends, and attending networking events to make new ones. We think of those activities as good and healthy, but they're actually remarkably unnatural, not to mention not very fun. Because if you saw a kid doing any of those things, you would feel like you were in an alternate universe. Kids don't run to stay fit, they run to feel the wind on their face and the grass beneath their feet. Kids don't network to climb a career ladder, they bond through joyful moments. Kids go for what they want without worrying about why or what for—they just want to have fun. As adults, we deny ourselves that luxury without understanding the incredible benefits we're missing out on.

Physical play is a powerful driver of your brain's plasticity (its ability to change and learn), especially when it challenges your balance and makes you move in new ways. Even simple games force you to consider a wide variety of possible outcomes and make quick decisions. That engages and strengthens your prefrontal cortex, i.e., your "executive function." You get to explore those possibilities in a low-stakes environment, where the consequences of making poor choices aren't serious.

Playing with others is also critical for developing and refining social skills. It teaches you how to cooperate, read emotions, and express yourself. The basis of human trust is established through play signals, and if we stop playing, we begin to lose those signals.[36]

This stuff is super important for kids, but it's still valuable in adulthood. Some of the most famous creatives in history—artists, inventors, writers—are notable for the importance they placed on play throughout their lives. Play boosts creativity because it keeps your sense of exploration and possibilities alive, and it reminds you that it's okay to test different ideas and approaches to a problem. Even in a competitive situation, maintaining a spirit of playfulness will help you perform your best because it takes focus off the stakes and opens up your creativity.

Play is also a powerful tool for shaping your identity as an adult. When you're young, your brain cells are hyperconnected, which makes it easy to learn and change. By age 25, nearly half of those connections are gone, and it takes more effort to create new connections or remove unwanted ones. Because play activates brain plasticity, it can help you change for the better throughout your life.

Brain health is one reason to play, but the other big one is simple: it's fun! Who doesn't want more fun in their life?

Hustle culture might be whispering in your ear right now, telling you that anything that's not productive is a waste of time. Something else is always more important, and there's always more to do than you seem to have time for. How can you justify adding playtime to your calendar? What are you, five?

Not only does that attitude suck the fun out of life, but

it also dampens the joy you feel when you *do* play because you're simultaneously judging yourself for slacking off.

It's also misguided. Play is a form of self-care.[37] It relieves stress, energizes you, lifts you out of the mundane, eases your burdens, and renews your optimism. By refreshing your mind, play actually makes you *more* productive when you get back to work—just like resting your muscles after a workout lets them heal and grow stronger.

Play also leads you to explore new behaviors, thoughts, strategies, and ways of being. It prompts you to look at things differently, which stimulates learning and creativity. Giving your brain a break from the problems it has been focused on can, paradoxically, lead to breakthroughs on those problems.

You thought you couldn't afford to play, but, it turns out, you actually can't afford not to.

When you make time for play, you'll see that the act of playing is just the start. Once you get into the habit, the play mindset will start to filter into your worldview. You'll feel more active, more adventurous, more free. It's like flipping your mind to a completely new channel.

That's when you'll start to lose tolerance for activities that don't bring you joy—and that's a good thing. The more fun you have in your life, the more you want to have, and you can bring that playful perspective to everything you do, including your work.

I like the sound of that.

Get In Your Time Machine

One day in your past, you had the last sleepover with your childhood friends, you just didn't realize it. The last time you played hide and seek. The last time you pranked your parents. The last time you had a snowball fight. But why?

We asked 20,000 people, "What's an experience you did as a child that you'd love to do again?" Here are some examples of what they said:

"Growing up I loved chasing around and catching fireflies in mason jars." —Terry, Indianapolis

"I miss having birthday parties at a rollerskating rink with pizza and cake." —Ryan, San Diego

"My favorite childhood tradition was dressing up as superheroes on Halloween and Trick or Treating at my neighbors' houses." —Jackson, Oklahoma City

"I loved believing in make believe characters like Santa and the Tooth Fairy. I miss that sense of wonder!" —Kameron, Sacramento

"When I'm driving, I usually just listen to the news or podcasts. But playing games like i-spy and road sign bingo on a road trip were so much more fun than that." —Blaire, Madison

"Playing laser tag with my brother was my favorite when I was a kid!" —Jillian, Knoxville

"I used to love obstacle courses as a child. I'd love to find a giant ball pit to dive into again!" —Charlie, Louisville

"I miss staying up all night telling ghost stories with s'mores at sleepaway camp!" —Charlene, Seattle

What do all of these answers have in common? They are all free or cheap and were so memorable that they came to mind right away, even after decades of originally doing them. They could also all be done still—no need to be a kid. And I promise, as an adult, they'd be more fulfilling than meeting up for a coffee, happy hour, or a Zoom catch up.

Six Ways to Play

So, how are you going to bring more play into your life? The options are endless, but let's take some inspiration from our survey—here are the top six types of experiences people said they missed about being a kid and wanted more of in their lives now.

COMPETE FOR LOW STAKES

The Pizza Wine tasting wasn't the only time I've incorporated a little friendly competition into a party. In fact, it's sort of a habit. Just last year, I threw a black tie party (yes, ball gowns and tuxedos required). Not just any black tie party, though—a Black Tie Baked Potato party where every guest was automatically entered into a competition to build the most beautiful and creative baked potato. The winner received a sack of potatoes.

Low-stakes competition is like a magic fun pill, which is why it's an essential element in any game. Remember those recess games, like tag, hide and seek, and four square? How about the sleepover games, like charades, flashlight tag, or a pillow fight? Or Connect Four, rock paper scissors, or Uno you might play on a family trip? In what could have been dull moments, those games sparked energy and laughter.

So, next time you're choosing what to do with your friends, partner, or kids, pick a game instead of a movie or a restaurant. It can be as simple as a board game or as elaborate as a full-scale obstacle course—or a Black Tie Baked Potato party. Have a yodeling contest. Host a drunken adult spelling bee. Play Twister. Have a pumpkin carving "art" show. See who is the best at lip syncing "I Will Always Love You." Whether you're facing off against each other or collaborating to beat the game itself, that friendly competition will revive your playfulness and make the moment one to remember.

You can even gamify your chores and other not-so-fun tasks. Set a timer and challenge yourself to complete a specific chore or task within a certain time frame. Try to beat your previous record and turn it into a friendly competition with yourself. Pretend to be a character or persona while doing chores with another person. Imagine yourself as a superhero or secret agent. Get creative and make up a mission related to your chores as you complete them and see who wins. The "loser" has to do the chore the next time. Why not? It adds a little spark of fun to an otherwise boring task.

CREATE WITHOUT EXPECTATION

A few years ago, I did something I hadn't done since I was a kid: I helped put on a play. Not a serious play—not something with weeks of rehearsals and a real theater and tickets and all that. No, this was a 90-minute affair from start to finish, including the writing, rehearsal, and performance.

It was the end of the week after I had spent dozens of hours exploring my inner child and bonding with my fellow participants at a mental health retreat. The activity was simple: write and perform a skit about our experience. Not something I would normally do for fun. But it *was* fun—so much that I wrote in my journal that night in big bold letters, "This was one of the best days of my entire life. *Never forget this day*." And I haven't.

Making things is a powerful way to play. Go back to your favorite arts and crafts materials: paper, colored pencils, paint, clay, glue, sparkles, whatever strikes your fancy. Make something, anything! Paper plate masks, handprint art, dyed eggs, macaroni necklaces, friendship bracelets. Make up a game. It sounds complicated, but kids do it all the time—they just pick some rules and figure out the rest as they go. Invite some friends over, play it, and see what happens. Create a jingle, a puppet show, a talent show...

whatever you want. It doesn't have to be "good" (whatever that means)—just enjoy the process.

Creating—especially when you do it just for fun, without the pressure of goals or expectations—taps into your imagination and helps you reconnect with your inner child. And who knows? You might even discover new abilities you didn't know you had.

EXPLORE THE GREAT OUTDOORS

When I look back at my own childhood, what I'm most grateful for is the freedom I had to explore. To be among nature and play with frogs, chase ducks, swim in ponds, ice skate, build snowmen, and jump in puddles. I wasn't constantly supervised, I wasn't tied to a screen, and my worth wasn't tied to likes on an app or grades on a paper. I was just outside exploring the natural world.

In my adult life, I try to do that as much as possible. In fact, my goal this year is to get dirty every day—a virtual guarantee that I'll spend a good chunk of my time outside. According to the Environmental Protection Agency, the average American spends 93 percent of their life indoors. That's only one-half of one day per week outdoors. Depressing! But that means you have the power to easily be above average.

Exploring means seeking to discover something. It means looking for something new and interesting, even in a familiar context. It means taking the time to notice details, try different paths, and savor the freedom of wandering around—literally or figuratively—with no particular end goal in mind.

Young children do this by default. With every new environment or object, they want to test out every aspect of it—where it starts and ends, what it feels like, what it contains, what it does. As you grow up, that open curiosity fades, partly because you get more focused on goal-oriented activities, but also because you take the familiar for granted. You think you've already learned everything that's worth knowing...but there's always more to discover.

Have fun in your own backyard, local park, or national park. See any sturdy trees with low hanging branches? Enjoy the thrill of climbing it. If you can find a vine, swing like Tarzan and let out a loud yell. Set up an obstacle course using natural elements—incorporate activities like climbing over fallen logs, balancing on tree stumps, crawling under branches, or jumping over small streams. Go on a treasure hunt to find interesting rocks, and display them in your home as souvenirs. Spend an evening laying on the hood of your car or in a tent stargazing and see what constellations you can spot. Get out on a river, lake, or ocean and play with floaties. Wear seaweed as a wig. Put on some goggles and chase schools of fish. Play Marco Polo and have a belly flop contest. Set up a slip and slide. Or simply jump in a puddle after a big rain.

Exploring nature with your own five senses is plenty of fun, but if you want to get really into it, there are plenty of tools and communities to take it to the next level. You can invest in cameras, binoculars, and telescopes to help you see things more clearly. You can even join a group of fellow birdwatchers, foragers, stargazers, entomologists, geologists, or whatever nature niche strikes your fancy. I am particularly fascinated with rocks, so I joined a community of women called Stone Studies (also affectionately referred to as "stoners"). We've traveled to places as far away as Hydra, Greece, and as close as Point Dume, Santa Barbara, and Big Sur, California, to immerse ourselves in areas that have unique and interesting stones and challenge ourselves to get creative with the elements. I use an app called Rock Identifier, and now have a whole rock collection that I proudly show off to visitors, whether they want to see them or not. By fostering a love for nature and providing opportunities for outdoor play, we develop a deeper connection with each other, our inner child, and the numerous health benefits nature offers.

LAUGH OUT LOUD

A few years ago, my mom, aunt, and cousin came to visit San Francisco and I took them whale watching, on what was quite possibly the foggiest day of the year. We saw a grand total of exactly zero whales. Instead of being sad about the whale-less experience, we all wrote bad haikus about the whales we didn't see, and then recited them for one another while mimicking the movements of a whale (or as I referred to mine, interpretive dancing). The winner of the haiku contest got a $3 plastic whale toy and their haiku framed, presented, and read aloud to everyone at our next family gathering. Laughing hysterically was a far more memorable bonding experience than actually seeing a whale.

When you laugh, you let go of your inhibitions and allow yourself to be silly and carefree—the very essence of play. Laughter has also been shown to relieve stress, decrease blood pressure, enhance oxygen intake, and stimulate your heart and other vital organs.

You don't have to wait until a family gathering or even until you get off work. At my old office at Universal, my friend and I made an enter-to-win box for our coworkers to try to "win" the chance to take us out to Benihana, complete with a badly photoshopped image of us in front of a Benihana. I'm sadly still waiting on that meal, but the 15 minutes that it took to put it together and place it on the receptionist's desk for everyone to see was one of my most memorable moments in that office because we laughed so hard.

So, find ways to laugh—and make others laugh—every day. Tell a joke, or write one of your own. Wear a costume in public. Go to a café with friends and have everyone make up life stories about the other patrons there. Dress up your puppy as a turkey on Thanksgiving. Rent a bounce house at your birthday party. Never be afraid to laugh at yourself. A good sense of humor can cure a bad mood and lighten the day for everyone around you.

BREAK THE RULES

Fourteen years ago, I went with four of my friends to get our photo taken with Santa at the Burbank mall. Were we far too old to be doing this? Absolutely. Did we care that we were the only group in line that did not include young children?

Nope. Is Santa kinda creepy with five grown women sitting on his lap? Definitely...which makes it even more hilarious. What was meant to be a one-time joke turned out to be so fun that it became an annual tradition, complete with themes and costumes. Even as our own families and lives grow and change, it's a once-a-year event where we can feel like kids again with each other.

A bit of harmless flouting of expectations is an excellent formula for fun. Kids know this—they're forever pushing the boundaries of the rules precisely for this reason. So, serve dessert before dinner. Jump in the pool fully dressed. Have a food fight. Break out into an impromptu dance in a public place. Jump on your bed. Have a pillow fight. Buy Nerf guns and chase around your friends. Why not? It's fun—it makes you feel alive and young.

Rebelling doesn't necessarily have to involve breaking the law or engaging in harmful behavior. It can be as simple as trying something that you've always been told you couldn't or shouldn't do, or expressing yourself in a way that feels authentic to you but may be unconventional. Like dressing up in tiaras, going to the mall, and sitting on Santa's lap, no matter how old you are.

PLAY A PRANK

Pranks can provide a much-needed break from the seriousness and stress of daily life. Once, my family and I went to pick up my cousin from the airport, and we made up an elaborate story about how she was the most famous kazoo player in the world...unbeknownst to her. We showed up at the airport terminal with giant handmade signs, kazoos, and Sharpies—and when she arrived, we all screamed like we were meeting a teenage heart throb. Everyone else waiting to pick up their friends or family genuinely thought she was famous—mission accomplished.

There's no need to bully people or do mean pranks, but when done in good humor and with respect for others, they can help develop resilience and the ability to handle unexpected situations...and be hilarious. So don't wait for April Fool's Day. Place a fake spider or snake where your target least expects it. Replace family photos with pictures of celebrities and see how long it takes for people to notice. Attach an air horn or whoopie cushion to someone's office chair. Rearrange the stuffed animals at Target to look like they're "having a good time." Prank call your friends from an unknown number and tell them their refrigerator is running. Put googly eyes on fruits at the grocery store. Or just do the classic jump-from-behind-a-door prank (to someone without heart problems, please).

Stay In Touch With Your Inner Child

Engaging in play is about more than just having fun. It's about rediscovering the sense of curiosity, openness, imagination, wonder, and carefree enjoyment that kids embody so naturally. That's our most natural and authentic state as humans.

So, it's worth doing a few small things to stay in touch with your childhood self. These are simple techniques that help you reconnect with the joys of that time, discover a more authentic version of yourself, and ultimately improve your overall well-being.

- **Childhood Photos:** Put a photo of you as a child somewhere you will see it often. It's a reminder to reflect on your younger self and let the childish side of you out more often. I have a photo on my fridge of my sister and me as little kids in the woods with deer antlers on our heads—a reminder of where my love of nature began.

- **Childhood Music:** Sound is an incredibly powerful way to conjure up memories. Think about a song you loved when you were younger. Listen to it today and try to remember the first time you heard it, or memories associated with that music. What other artists or songs had a major influence on your youth? Build a playlist and have fun listening to nostalgia. And don't try to act cool—the cheesier the better. My friends and I put Backstreet Boys and Celine Dion videos on the TV while we have parties. It brings us right back to our childhood.

- **Childhood Movies:** Get some popcorn and have a movie night with your favorite film from childhood. You may be surprised at how good—or bad—that movie is now. I once had a date where we both bought recorders (the $5 musical instrument), ran around like velociraptors, and wore dinosaur onesies to watch *Jurassic Park*...and perform the theme song of the movie for each other. I've been on (and forgotten) a lot of dates, and even though this one didn't work out, I'll always fondly remember it. And *Jurassic Park* is still 10/10.

- **Childhood Food**: Our senses trigger strong links to memories and emotions, and foods are especially powerful because they combine sight, smell, and taste. Think of a comfort food or meal from your childhood. What about it makes you sentimental? Who does it remind you of? Try to recreate it, and let it take you back to those times in your mind. When I was a kid, my grandma would make my cousins and me her "famous" macaroni and cheese. When we got older, we realized it was just Velveeta, butter, and shells—not exactly a health food, but we recreated it together and giggled at how we used to think it was the epitome of fine dining.

- **Childhood Home**: Visualize your childhood home and bedroom. Take a virtual walk down your childhood street on Google Maps, and see if your house is still there. Do the same with your elementary school. See if that jogs any fun memories that you may have forgotten. Think about and imagine yourself as an eight-year-old. What would you say to that kid now?

- **Childhood Toys:** It doesn't seem quite fair that only kids are supposed to have toys. I loved Super Soakers when I was young, so I got a few for the summer to play with my friends. It doubles as a fun way to wash my windows and get weird looks from my neighbors. Win-win. Bonus points if you find an old toy from your childhood on eBay.

- **Childhood Party:** Host an adult slumber party, complete with pillow forts, kid snacks, and a nostalgic theme. I've had a Teenage Mutant Ninja Turtle themed party as both a child and adult—and I promise, my friends remember that one more than a typical dinner party.

- **Childhood Dreams:** When you ask a kid what they want to do when they grow up, it's usually something like "I want to be an astronaut, a firefighter, a baseball star." Those professions make them excited and curious. But then the world wears them down quickly and tells them they can't do it, that it's impossible, and that they should take the safe route instead. When you were young, what did you want to be or do when you grew up? Is there a way you can do that or get close to it, even temporarily? If you wanted to be a firefighter, look into volunteering at the local station. If you used to dress up as an astronaut for Halloween, go to space camp. If you dreamed of being a baseball player, join a league or organize some friends to play one night. Let your inner child experience the thing they dreamed of.

These simple actions will help bring your inner child into focus and keep them at the forefront of your mind. They'll remind you to stay open, be curious, and keep on playing. Life can be very serious. It's good to let some pressure out of the valve sometimes.

You're a Big Kid Now

If you haven't guessed already, I'm basically an overgrown kid. I mean, I'm the person who has held birthday parties at Chuck E. Cheese and Sky Zone Trampoline Parks...not so long ago. That may sound ridiculous, but this attitude has given me some of the very best times of my life—moments full of uncontrollable laughter, even in the most ordinary circumstances. I didn't have to go anywhere special or spend much or any money to have them. I just had to give myself the time, space, and permission to play.

As adults, we schedule ourselves wall to wall, and we tend to fill the gaps with "practical" things or waste them on mindless screen time. But if you can reframe play as something you need—something that's good for you, that you should be proud to do—you'll find that you can turn even the most routine days into experiences worth remembering.

✦ ✦ ✦

EXERCISE

Go Play

Take a few minutes to think and journal on these questions:

1. Think back on your childhood. What were your favorite ways to play? How did they make you feel? Spend 5-10 minutes visualizing those memories in as much detail as possible.

2. When did you stop doing those things, and why?

3. In your life today, are there any activities you do purely for fun, with no goals or expectations about the outcome? If not, why?

4. What's one play activity you'd like to do more of? How can you give yourself the time, space, and permission to do it?

5. Schedule time to do that activity.

Note: Go to ExperientialBillionaire.com *to download or print an extended version of this exercise in addition to free experience guides.*

Chapter Nine

UNLOCK THE VAULT

OF LIFELONG LEARNING

"The more that you read, the more you will know, the more that you learn, the more places you'll go."

—Dr. Seuss

Joe:

After my dad moved to Mexico, I started visiting him a few times a year. It was fun to hang out with him and his expat friends, but they were mostly older gringos (used affectionately) whose preferred physical activity was "happy hour." I, on the other hand, was a fit twenty-something thrill seeker. I wanted to experience the adventurous side of San Carlos with people around my own age and fitness level. (And, of course, go to the bars where the pretty girls hung out, not the yacht club full of expat retirees who definitely did not own yachts.)

There was one obstacle though: Spanish. Every time I met other people who were doing the things I wanted to be doing, they barely spoke English, and I spoke just about zero Spanish. (Unless you count, "*Dónde está la biblioteca?*"—thanks, freshman year Spanish class!)

So, I decided to learn. I didn't have time for a class, but I was driving a lot for work, and the drive to visit my dad was 14 hours. I bought CDs that were literally called "Learn Spanish in Your Car," and that's what I did. For hours and hours and hours, all I listened to was Spanish. I learned basic nouns, then verbs, and eventually even tenses. There wasn't a lot of room in my life for practicing real conversations, so I just sort of kept absorbing it.

After a few months, I went back down to my dad's, and something magical happened. A bilingual friend invited me to the opening of a new bar, where he introduced me to some girls who immediately started speaking to me in rapid-fire Spanish (what had previously sounded like staccato gunfire to my ears). As I stood there staring with a silly grin on my face, I slowly realized I could understand what they were saying. Not all of it, but enough to communicate and make friends—and it was *awesome*. Suddenly, I was able to be a part of a whole new world. (Cue *The Little Mermaid* soundtrack.)

To be clear, my Spanish wasn't (and still isn't) great. It's a C- that improves to a solid B with a little tequila and some unfounded confidence. But what had started out with me simply trying to order a beer and find a bathroom evolved into a strong desire to become more fluent and gain a deeper understanding of Spanish-speaking cultures. I'm still learning, but my experience with Spanish inspired me to add some Italian, French, and a little (very little) Arabic to my secret agent skills resumé. The learning process itself is a gratifying experience, and those languages have opened the door to even more experiences—things that would never have happened had I stuck to my native language.

When you learn a new language, suddenly there's a whole new population of people you can interact with—millions of people who can now be your friends, lovers, teachers, colleagues, clients, and more. You can move around in their world more easily, which makes travel to those places full of possibility. You can experience their culture firsthand, expanding your worldview and potentially your lifestyle. Even if you just start with the goal of learning just a few short phrases, you never know where it will take you (hopefully somewhere with beer and a bathroom).

When it comes to learning, Mahatma Gandhi put it best: "Live as if you'll die tomorrow, learn as if you were to live forever." In other words, cultivate a sense of urgency to pursue your desires and dreams *now*, but don't let that stop you from investing in your long-term growth.

When we're young, we're constantly learning. Somewhere along the line, that growth starts to wane. We finish school (barely, in my case), and there's no longer someone handing us assignments to learn stuff. We figure out who we are, master (or become somewhat passable at) the basics of adulthood, and settle into a career. By the time we hit our thirties, the pace of learning has dropped off a cliff. By middle age, it has slowed to a crawl. That feels peaceful, in a way. We don't have the constant stress of not knowing what to do or how to handle things.

But it's also boring as hell, not to mention a waste. We only get one life to explore this world and make the most of ourselves. As Albert Einstein once said, "Once you stop learning, you start dying."

Metaphorical death aside, the benefits of being a lifelong learner are vast. It feels good, helps you discover your talents, expands your world, is a great social activity, keeps you healthy, and creates value for you and others. Sound familiar? It should. The benefits of learning are very similar to the benefits of having meaningful experiences. That's because learning is by nature a meaningful experience.

In our global *Life Experience Survey*, when we asked participants what they wanted to learn in their lifetimes, the results were as follows:

1. Learn a musical instrument (guitar, piano, etc.): **31%**
2. Learn a new language (Spanish, French, etc.): **25%**
3. Learn a new sport (tennis, surfing, snowboarding, etc.): **11%**
4. Learn to cook (Thai, Japanese, etc.): **10%**
5. Learn to make art (paint, sculpt, draw, etc.): **5%**
6. Learn to fly or drive (plane, racecar, boat, etc.): **4%**
7. Learn to dance (salsa, ballroom, ballet, etc.): **2%**
8. Learn to build (house, woodworking, carpentry, etc.): **2%**
9. Various other: **10%**

Then, we asked why they hadn't done it yet. A whopping 66 percent of people said they just hadn't gotten around to it. Hadn't made time for it. Hadn't made it a priority. Here are examples of what they said:

"My dream is to learn how to sing and perform for my friends and family." —Sal, Las Vegas

"I always wanted to learn my family's native language (Japanese) to be able to communicate better with them." —Ann, San Diego

"I wish I had learned how to cook better when my kids were still living in our house so I could have taught them our old family recipes." —Molly, Bay City

"I always thought learning how to rebuild cars like my dad did would be so cool and a way to bond with him." —Jay, Atlanta

"I grew up by a lake and I never learned ice skating, but now that I'm getting older, I'm worried if I waited too long." —Disha, Muskegon

Don't make that mistake. Learning isn't just for young people. It's the best way to keep your mind agile and explore your full potential as a human being, throughout your life. That's why it's so important to incorporate rich learning experiences into your life, at any age.

How to Be a Lifelong Learner

You don't have to go back to school or invest an unreasonable amount of time or money to start expanding your knowledge, skills, hobbies, and interests. This section outlines how to get started and back on track.

BE A BEGINNER AGAIN

There's obvious value in deepening the skills and expertise you already use in your everyday life. Many adults take classes, go to conferences, or read literature in their primary area of expertise. Sometimes it's even required, if you're in an industry that has mandatory professional development, like medicine or teaching. You might even go back to school for an advanced degree in hopes of securing a pay raise or promotion.

But there's a different kind of value in learning brand new things—not just new facts but new *skills*. Being a beginner again.

That might not sound very attractive to you. Plenty of people have not-so-fond memories of beginnerhood—of endless struggles, of feeling stupid, of exasperated teachers and bullying peers. Now, as an adult, you imagine it would be the same. You expect to feel hapless and inept, and anyone watching would judge you as a dilettante—not worthy of being taken seriously. After all, don't serious people have better things to do than flail around ineffectually with a golf club, a paintbrush, or a keyboard they *clearly* don't know how to use?

That's some modern-era bullshit. "Dilettante" comes from an Italian word meaning "to delight," which is exactly how it should feel to dabble in various pursuits simply because you want to. Doing so used to be a privilege of the wealthy, which is why there's still a stigma among busy, hardworking people in today's "hustle culture" that hobbies are silly and frivolous—a sign that you have too much time on your hands.[38] Why bother starting something new if you'll never be great at it? Wouldn't it be wiser to use that time to double down on skills you already use?

Even our language reflects society's collective opinion of beginners. We give them derogatory names: "kook," "newbie, "rookie," "amateur"—all have negative connotations, to varying degrees.

Babies don't suck at walking. They just don't know how yet. They aren't bad at talking; they just haven't learned the words and picked up the skills yet. When it comes to learning, we need to all get over ourselves and our pride and realize it's okay to be a beginner and learn from scratch. Eventually we'll walk and talk, but first it's going to be a bit of falling and goo goo ga ga. Baby steps.

I definitely did a bit of falling when I learned how to skate a vert ramp. My friends had skated backyard ramps when I was growing up, but I missed the party because, well, I was actually partying. I had always envied them for the fun they were having that I was excluded from. So, when I moved to the beach, instead of becoming focused on surfing as one might expect, I started skateboarding every day. It took me years to progress from cruising neighborhood streets to exploring my abilities (aka flailing about) at skate parks to finally getting up the nerve to drop in for the first time. I'll never forget that adrenaline-filled moment, staring down past my board as it hung precariously over the 12-foot ledge. Leaning over and committing. Those moments of vertical free fall, the brief feeling of weightlessness before the press of gravity and rush of speed up the other side. That was on my 30th birthday—far later than I'm guessing most people have that experience. It may have taken me a couple decades longer than my childhood friends, but the experience was just as magical.

I still skate ramps now, because as Jay Adams of Dogtown and Z-Boys fame said, "You didn't stop skating because you got old. You got old because you stopped skating." I can't begin to describe the amount of joy skateboarding has provided, aside from the side benefits of fitness, fresh air, vitamin D, and a more in-depth look at all my local surroundings. Of all the things I'm most excited about as a parent, teaching my kids the joy of skateboarding is definitely among the highest. The beauty of loving something that you're constantly learning to get better at is that it's fun at every level. I'm no Tony Hawk, to be sure, but I'm also sure I love skateboarding just as much as Tony does.

FOCUS ON YOUR PERSONAL PROGRESS

You don't have to become an expert for the learning to have value. The process can be enjoyable and create benefits at any level, even when you're a novice.

In fact, the value in the experience of learning something is not tied to how good or proficient you are, but instead lies in your own personal relationship with the thing you are learning. Your perspective dictates your experience, which is why one person can feel as much joy from running a 5K as another will feel after completing an ultramarathon—and why there was a time I felt the same joy and exhilaration riding off the curb in front of my house as the pros felt doing the "Big Air Contest" at the X Games. Once you remove the fear of not being great at something, you can enjoy it at any level in the learning process.

Since joy comes from making progress, it's important to design your learning in a way that gives you a string of small successes that require significant effort to achieve. If there's too much failure between those successes, you'll feel stalled and get discouraged. On the other hand, if success comes too easily, you'll get bored.

You want to stay in the Goldilocks Zone: not too hard, not too easy, but just right.[39] That's the zone where you learn the fastest and enjoy it most. If I would have tried to drop in on a vert ramp when I first started skating, I would have just face-planted straight to the bottom of the ramp and most likely seriously injured myself. Likewise, had I never left the neighborhood sidewalk, I would have gotten bored and hung up my skateboard for good. Learning the basic fundamentals and progressing step by step got me from the sidewalk to the vert ramp—and I had a blast the entire way.

Doing something poorly over and over with no discernible improvement is tedious (and painful). When you break it down the Goldilocks way, you get a string of tiny victories that feels so rewarding. The baby steps are small enough to actually achieve, so you make real progress much faster, and you can feel it happening.

On the reward side, people tend to underestimate the joy of making progress. You don't have to wait until you're great at something to have fun; each step brings fulfillment. The journey is the destination, and no matter how far you go, you're never done, because there's no finish line. You can always take another step, and the joy of that step will be the same as the ones that came before.

If you repeatedly tell yourself that making an error means you're *about* to make progress, your brain can learn to actually make you feel good about those errors. Whenever you're feeling frustrated with a learning task, remind yourself, "This is good for me. It's a sign of growth. I'm on the right track."

Growing up, I never played team sports. I always felt I missed out on that team experience, so once I moved to the beach I recruited some of my surfer friends and we formed a team, the Fern Street Pigs, to join the local adult's softball league. We thought it would be some lighthearted fun, only to find that the other teams were full of fanatics who had been playing since childhood and were very serious about the games and results. We lost every single game the first season, except the last one, and you would have thought we'd won the World Series by how we celebrated that one single win (even though we were still dead last in the league). I still have the bar tab for proof.

The experience bonded us, though, and we had so much fun that we actually practiced a few times in the off-season and figured out who should play each position (yeah, does seem obvious in hindsight). The next season, we improved so much that we won every game and the whole league. It was definitely a fun time, but interestingly, we didn't really have more fun than the previous year. It's not the being good that feels rewarding—it's the getting better.

FIND A GUIDE

To get started with any new activity you want to learn, some type of experienced teacher, mentor, or coach can kick-start your experience and shave months or even years off your learning curve. Because, unlike play, which has no goal or expectations, the idea of learning is to actually *get better* over time. Complete mastery might not be the end goal, but progress is the whole point of any learning journey.

When you successfully learn something new, even if it's just a tiny baby step forward from your current skill level, your brain rewards you. It gives you a little hit of pleasure to encourage you to keep at it. That's why learning is so fulfilling. It's literally like taking a drug. It releases that feel-good hit of dopamine that tells our body and mind that this is good stuff.

If you're thinking, *Yeah right, learning was always miserable for me*, then you were probably stuck in a failure rut for too long, too many times. You didn't have enough of those moments of mastery to get you through the frustration of all the missed attempts. That doesn't mean you suck at learning, or learning will never be fun for you. It just means there was a learning design problem. The challenge wasn't broken down into small enough steps, they weren't in the right order, or you weren't getting the right feedback to guide your efforts in the right direction. A good teacher, preferably one who works with beginners, can solve all those issues.

Most people, if they haven't been taught how to practice, will simply start doing things—playing a song on guitar, downhill skiing, or drawing a face—and fumble through it for as much time as they have available, or until they get frustrated or bored. This approach, while better than nothing, might not produce very much learning, and it can possibly even do the opposite: by allowing yourself to repeatedly make the same mistakes without correcting them, you might actually be learning to do it wrong.

There's nothing more effective than getting real-time feedback from a real human being, especially when you're just starting out. It can be a friend, colleague, or paid instructor. Don't assume you don't have access to world-class teachers—people who have reached the highest levels of their profession—for whatever is at the top of your list, whether it's free diving, songwriting, or Olympic ice broom shuffleboarding (I refuse to call it curling—makes no sense). The cost is often much less than you'd think and the value much more.

Because beginners in any activity tend to all make the same errors, which are well-known and easy to correct. In drawing, beginners overemphasize features that are important in their minds—like eyes—instead of drawing what they actually see. In skiing, they tend to lean too far back and look at the front of the skis instead of ahead of them. In skydiving, they forget to pack a parachute (this is usually a one-time mistake). A coach or mentor know the classic errors and how to correct them before they generate too much frustration, or worse, become bad habits that you later have to unlearn.

Sometimes, though, working with a teacher isn't possible or practical. In that case, look for a course, book, or software program that's up-to-date and designed for beginners like you. I recently did that with guitar, which I've been "learning" to play since I was a teenager. I'm pretty terrible (a C- that only gets *worse* with tequila), but I enjoy playing and find it very cathartic, even though I can barely play a few dozen songs after all these years. Just in the last year, I signed up for an online course and started doing 15 minutes a day, four days a week. In the first few months so far, I've learned scales I never knew, several new songs, and some great riffs that make my impromptu jamming sound way more legit. Plus, this progress has made me even more excited to share my passion for music with my kids. My goal is to perform a song on stage by the end of 12 months. It doesn't matter if it's a coffee shop, a kid's birthday party, or *Saturday Night Live* (call me, Lorne)—I just want to perform a song on a stage in front of people at least once in my life. And guess what? A year of instruction only cost me $95. (I paid for the whole year up front to hold myself accountable, *à la* "self-imposed consequences.")

PRACTICE ACTIVE LEARNING

Once you understand the basic fundamentals, you need to start actually doing the thing you want to learn. Reading about skills can provide a foundational understanding. Actively doing things is crucial for faster and more effective learning. By engaging in hands-on practice, you benefit from experiential learning, muscle memory development, learning from mistakes, contextual understanding, and confidence building. Growth and improvement comes from a combination of theory and practice.

According to research, the act of doing things greatly increases our retention and subsequent growth. Just reading about something or watching tutorials won't have much effect unless you actually try to do the thing. You're not going to become a great gardener if you don't get your hands dirty. You're not going to get good at free throws if you don't go outside and throw up some shots. You're not going to become a concert pianist if you don't sit down at the piano and bang on the keys a bit each day.

Physically doing something trains your body and mind to work together, resulting in improved coordination, reflexes, and overall performance—no matter what that thing is. You learn from what works and what doesn't. You take the knowledge of how the thing you're learning works and then experiment, make mistakes, and iterate. It's important to research and learn, but much more important to take that knowledge and actually put it into practice. No one ever read about how to ride a bike and then got on one and rode away on the first try.

COMPOUND YOUR EFFORTS

Another important element of the learning process is how often you engage in it and for how long. Practicing something new is mentally taxing because it requires intense focus to vigilantly catch and correct errors, over and over. Research advises spending 10 to 30 minutes a day on this kind of learning.[40] If you have the energy for it, you can do multiple cycles of this in a day, but allowing your brain to rest is a vital part of building new neural pathways.

If you want to make progress quickly and efficiently, spending a little time learning every day is the way to go. It's much better than setting aside several hours once a week, or a whole day once a month. Our brains can't endure that much practice at once; so much of that time will be used ineffectively, and the long stretches in between make it harder to retain what we've learned. Anything past an hour of practice for a new activity or skill, whether it's mentally strenuous or physically challenging, takes us way beyond the improvement zone and the rate of diminishing returns goes up dramatically. Being consistent in small daily doses is much better than lengthy but sporadic bursts of activity.

Also, the science is pretty clear that our brains encode what we learn during periods of rest, so learning every day gives us more rest and sleep periods to encode those things successfully, versus wasting six days a week and then trying to learn and encode everything all at once.

This applies to absorbing and retaining new information as well. For example, I've found immense value (and much higher retention levels) in short, daily bursts of learning with the "Great Courses" on Audible. I've used these incredible courses to study many things: Egypt, before I went to the Pyramids; London, as I spent more time there and wanted to understand it better; public speaking, as I started doing that professionally; the history of modern religions, before I started touring the Middle East; the American West, before I worked with Native American reservations on the Great Plains; and lots more. Each course is equivalent to a college semester of lectures on the topic of your choice and is taught by the best professors from the top universities in the world. The half-hour lessons allow me to soak up the knowledge of some of the brightest minds in the world while simply doing a drive to work, a workout, or other daily activity.

CULTIVATE A GROWTH MINDSET

We are the product of our own thoughts, and having the right mindset is crucial for lifelong learning. A "fixed mindset" is the view that our abilities are a reflection of inherent talent or intelligence and, as such, cannot be significantly changed or developed. A "growth mindset" is the belief that even if we struggle with certain skills, our abilities aren't set in stone, and with work, we can improve over time.

This simple distinction leads to completely different behaviors and emotional experiences during the learning process. If you have a fixed mindset, you'll view failure as a sign that you don't have what it takes to succeed. It will make you feel not only frustrated but also incompetent and hopeless, and you're likely to quit after a few unsuccessful attempts.

If you have a growth mindset, failing doesn't mean you *can't*—it just means you *haven't yet*. You need to adjust and try again, and maybe again and again and again. Repeated failure might feel frustrating, but you'll respond with determination and focus instead of hopelessness. You'll keep at it until you get it, and you'll celebrate your success as a true achievement when you do.

The fixed mindset also makes the whole idea of learning something new feel scary. If you believe your performance is a reflection of something inherent in you, the prospect of being an inept beginner will act as a threat to your ego. This (obviously) leads to a tendency to avoid challenges, give up easily in the face of obstacles, and ignore opportunities for growth and improvement.

With a growth mindset, you're free from that imagined threat. You know your ability comes through effort and practice. Your talents can be developed and improved through dedication, effort, and continuous learning. Who cares if you suck at first? Everyone sucks at first. If you work at it, you'll get better. Remember, think like a baby. You might need to keep trying, but eventually you'll walk.

Cultivating a growth mindset shifts the balance between perceived risk and reward during the learning process. Most people overestimate the risks of trying something new, which essentially boil down to being laughed at or criticized. In reality, others are not paying attention and don't care if you look silly. In fact, they'll probably admire you for trying.

BECOME A POLYMATH

It's okay to go deep on one topic, activity, or passion, but don't close the door to all the other things on offer. Human beings weren't meant to specialize in one area or one thing. Learning new things also expands your identity. It's an investment in yourself as a person, which not only makes your life more fulfilling but also makes you more interesting and valuable to other people. Curiosity, awareness, and eagerness to learn are very attractive qualities.

A polymath is someone with expertise in a diverse range of areas. People often use the word in a way that makes it sound like polymaths are born geniuses, but it actually comes from the Greek *polymathēs*, which simply means "having learned much."

We're all capable of becoming multi-disciplinary and (most) people have an innate desire to learn about a wide variety of things, but modern society pushes us to specialize in just one area. The logic is, the deeper your expertise in that area, the more valuable you are. But in reality, it makes you interchangeable. A master software engineer is easy to find, but what about one who is also an excellent team leader, a compelling public speaker, and conversant in the basics of graphic design? That person is irreplaceable. Each skill contributes to the others, in a mutually reinforcing web of skills that creates a unique, nuanced perspective on the world.

Plus, having many skills often makes it easier to learn new things. It's almost like a cheat. By having other experiences, you create advantages, so one plus one can sometimes equal three. The classic whole is greater than the sum of the parts. I picked up snowboarding and wakeboarding quickly because I was already pretty good at skateboarding. It was easy for me to learn some basic French and Italian because I was already conversational in Spanish. Once I started my first company, I knew how to start another new company, even though they operated in different industries. When we learn new things, we add small building blocks that can become the foundation for great things of major value in our future.

Old Dog, New Tricks

One of the reasons learning slows down as we age is because we get settled into our identities. We've lived enough to know what we're good at and what we're not, who we are and who we aren't—or so we think. It's easy to get caught up in those stories and not question them. For example, maybe you tell yourself you're not a good painter. You think, *I'm not original or artistic. I wasn't good at drawing when I was a kid, so I probably suck at painting too. I could never make something out of nothing. That's just not my thing.*

But...what if you're wrong? What if you just haven't tried the right thing the right way yet, or persisted with it for long enough to see what you're really capable of?

Maybe you have a knack for hat knitting, beer brewing, portrait photography, dog training, or some other thing you've never tried to learn before. The thing is, even if you do have a hidden talent or passion for something, it might not show up on first contact. You might have a great ear for music, but *no one* sounds good the first time they pick up an instrument, no matter how good their ear is. Trying new things is like getting more pieces to help you fill in the puzzle of your life.

For me, one of those puzzle pieces was writing. I had an idea a few years back (okay, it was a decade) for an epic fantasy adventure novel. I wrote out the idea on a page of my journal, and there it sat for a year or two. The idea continued to grow and percolate in my mind, but I had never written a book of any kind, much less something of that magnitude or scope, so I put off any serious attempt to write it. Then one day, a screenwriter friend of mine told me that great screenplays are sometimes written in just a week or two. I thought, *Screenplay? I could do that.*

Before I started, I read books and listened to some courses on writing. I downloaded a free version of software that writers use for screenplays and novels. I found samples online of my favorite action adventure movies like *Raiders of the Lost Ark*, printed them out, studied them, and made detailed notes on the plot points and on how they were structured. Learning those steps gave me the confidence to get started.

After a few weeks of plugging away in the screenplay format, I realized that I was definitely writing a novel, not a screenplay. I switched to novel mode and continued getting lost in the new fantasy world I was creating in my mind. The characters started taking on a life of their own. The story took turns and wound up places I never expected. It kept evolving, and so did I as it went on. The book turned into an epic tome that's nearly a thousand pages long, and along the way, "writer" became part of my identity.

Before I actually tried it, I definitely didn't consider myself a writer (unless you count my comedy routines about going bankrupt). Now I have not one but two books finished. When you try new things, you might find that some of your internal stories aren't true, or at least they're not set in stone. It turns out that most things, if you have the interest and intentionally put in time, are much more doable than you think. You just have to start. As I learned, you can always edit a bad page but you can't edit a blank page.

I would be lying if I said I won't get an immense amount of satisfaction from the publication of that novel (I'm willing to entertain all offers), but truth be told, the amount of joy I've already derived from the actual writing of it has been beyond rewarding. That's what art and learning is all about. Loving the act of learning, creating, being, doing. Not the result. If everyone in the world thinks my epic fantasy adventure sucks, I still had an amazing experience, and one that I can proudly tell my kids and parents and friends about. It doesn't matter if no one else ever reads it. I've re-read it many times and I love it. As they say, "Art is in the eye of the beholder."

I took lessons on trapeze, axe throwing, archery, breathwork, free diving, yoga, golf, and kiteboarding all throughout my thirties. I started mountain biking, backcountry snowboarding, and writing in my early forties. And just in the last year, I learned the invaluable skill of public speaking. They say you can't teach an old dog new tricks, but this old dog says that's bullshit.

The Golden Age of Learning

There's never been a better time to learn. You already know that music, languages, sports, and cooking were the top answers in our survey. Luckily, the rest of the answers gave us a treasure trove of ideas for other learning gems. Here are some ideas for your next skill—it's not a comprehensive list, but it's a great place to start.

- **Foraging:** Most people don't realize that no matter where you live, there are things to forage, even in urban environments. Go outside and find something edible—mushrooms, seaweed, berries, seeds, greens, shellfish, or flowers. Do your research to ensure it's safe to eat. Depending on the mushroom variety, you can have a delicious, mind-expanding, or lethal experience. Two of those are good for you. One, not so much.

- **Gardening:** Studies have found that gardening improves your mood and increases your self-esteem. Embrace your green thumb. Find a favorite fruit or vegetable that you can grow at home. Strawberries, blackberries, cucumbers, and carrots are all great places to start. Depending on your needs, grapes, hops, or barley could also come in handy. Plant it outside, in your kitchen, or windowsill and learn how to grow it.

- **Brewing:** Humans have been brewing things for time immemorial. Luckily, making your favorite beverage at home is likely easier than you think. Learn how to make your own wine, sake, kombucha, beer, tea, or roast your own coffee beans at home. For supplies, see "Gardening" above.

- **Survival Skills:** How long would you last in the wild (or the zombie apocalypse)? Learn how to build a fire, make shelter, treat a wound, scare off predators, and all the other skills that will keep you alive when civilization is out of reach. You'll gain a greater respect for wildlife and their habitats, as well as the ability to enjoy places that might be off-limits to less adventurous souls.

- **Self-Defense:** You don't have to be Bruce Lee to learn how to protect yourself and your companions. Pick a martial art to study, or take classes in basic self-defense techniques. Who knows—it might save your life one day.

- **Arts:** Get your creative juices flowing and sketch the view from your window, paint a watercolor of your favorite fruit, or take artistic photos of yourself and your family. Frame your art, and when people ask, tell them it's a famous artist and you got it in Paris at a gallery.

- **Crafts:** Making things with your hands can help you enter a flow state, where your mind is fully present and immersed in the activity. What are some things you could use or gift someone? Could be a keychain, candle, crochet, pottery, picture frame, jewelry, tote bag, or prison shank out of a toothbrush. Get creative and DIY something.

- **Writing:** Storytelling is an ancient and powerful tool that we all possess. Start by writing a short story or a poem about your most embarrassing moment or the strangest thing that ever happened to you. Challenge yourself to write a little every day, with different writing prompts to keep the ideas coming.

- **Speaking:** Public speaking is an important skill that is shown to boost confidence, improve critical thinking, and expand professional opportunities. A thoughtful toast at a dinner party or saying something special to a store clerk, barista, or coworker are great ways to practice without a stage or large audience.

- **Strategy Games:** Learning a strategy game supports the development of higher order thinking skills—like problem solving, decision making, critical thinking, planning, and even creativity. Pick up a set of chess, backgammon, mahjong, cribbage, or dominoes and set up a regular game with friends or family. You can even practice online to hone your skills so you can show your friends who's boss—and who doesn't want that?

- **Culture:** Understanding other cultures helps us overcome and prevent ideological divisions that can lead to misunderstandings, loss of opportunities, and violence. What cultures are around you that you don't know much about? Wikipedia is a surefire (and free) way to go deeper and will lead down rabbit holes that can help expand your appreciation for humanity. Even if you agree to disagree.

The options for learning are truly limitless. There are dozens of marketplaces for online courses and tutors, and they grow bigger every day. You can visit the Smithsonian Natural History Museum or Harvard's most popular classes for free, from your laptop. Nearly all the information and expertise in the world is at your fingertips (and anything that's not is probably classified). Thirty years ago, none of this was possible. We live in a time of endless learning opportunities—take advantage of it.

You Are What You Know

If you think you're too busy to pick up a new hobby, you need it even more than you realize. As you know by now, what people regret most at the end of life is what they didn't do—the person they didn't become. When you stop exploring that potential is when you open the door to regret.

That's why, whenever I think about all the things our participants said they wanted to learn in their lifetime, I'm a bit overcome with emotion. I know those answers—singing, magic tricks, Mandarin, martial arts, dancing, filmmaking, graphic design— aren't just text in a box. They're someone's dreams that are slipping away, one day at a time.

I'm reminded of this quote from Les Brown:

> The graveyard is the richest place on earth because it is here that you will find all the hopes and dreams that were never fulfilled, the books that were never written, the songs that were never sung, the inventions that were never shared, the cures that were never discovered, all because someone was too afraid to take that first step, keep with the problem, or determined to carry out their dream.

But it doesn't have to end this way. It's not too late. If you start now, your quote can be, "I had a chance, and I'm taking it, and I'm living life to the fullest."

So, instead of dreading learning, embrace it. Every time you learn something new, no matter how trivial or significant, you're investing in your own identity and making yourself into a wiser and more experienced version of you than you were the day before.

✦ ✦ ✦

EXERCISE

What's Your Next Skill?

Follow these simple steps to make learning part of your life again, starting now.

1. What's the number one thing you want to start learning? For inspiration, look at the Treasure Map you created in Chapter 1, or consider the activities mentioned in this chapter and throughout the book. What piques your interest?

2. Once you've decided what to pursue, plan it out. (Remember, writing down where and when you're going to do something makes you far more likely to actually do it.) Here are some important questions to answer:
   a. Who are you going to learn from? Find a teacher, course, software program, or book to guide you.
   b. When are you going to make time to spend on this? Try to engage in it at least once a week, if not more. Put it on your calendar.

c. Consider whether you need to adjust your budget or create a special savings pool to fund this learning experience.
d. Go out and get any gear or clothes you need to get started.

Taking these small steps now sets the entire process in motion and puts momentum on your side. Now you're on your way to becoming a lifelong learner.

Note: Go to ExperientialBillionaire.com *to download or print an extended version of this exercise in addition to free experience guides.*

Chapter Ten

“The purpose of life
is a life of purpose.”

—Robert Byrne

Bridget:

I squirmed as a thousand pinkish-orange fish nibbled at my bare feet. Apparently this was supposed to be a relaxing "massage," but it felt like tickle torture instead. We were at the southernmost tip of Sri Lanka, with nothing but ocean ahead for 6,000 miles to Antarctica. As I dangled my limbs in the warm water and contemplated a future without toes, I wondered, *How did I get here?*

The previous week, we had searched for snake charmers, devoured curry and egg hoppers, visited Buddhist temples, met with cinnamon farmers, taken shots of some sketchy moonshine out of a bathtub in the jungle, seen hatching babies at a sea turtle sanctuary, and taken shelter with monkeys in a mangrove forest after getting caught in a torrential downpour in a rowboat.

But we weren't there to have adventures––that was just a bonus. In fact, years later, reminiscing about that trip, those moments barely get a mention. We were there to work with soldiers from both sides of the Sri Lankan civil war, many of whom had lost their hearing during the 15-year conflict.

What we reminisce about is the family that traveled 20 hours on a bus to the military base in Colombo where we were stationed. We remember crying with them as they witnessed their four-year-old daughter hearing for the first time—something they never thought possible.

We talk about our dance-off to "Thriller" with a 13-year-old boy who could suddenly reconnect with his peers and the world around him. He wanted to be a performer like the ones he saw on TV, and being able to hear again meant everything to him.

We talk about the two guys in their early thirties who had previously been enemies but found common ground that day when sharing their experiences of the war.

We remember being humbled by the impact of seeing a hundred-year-old man as he suddenly became full of personality after not having sound in his life for 50 years.

These are just four stories out of more than 2,000 on that trip. We were lucky enough to touch their lives, and they touched ours—and there's no telling how much good may have flowed from those connections.

That four-year-old girl has now gone through years of school that she would have missed entirely if she were still unable to hear. The family might remember that moment as one that changed the course of their future, and pay it forward.

The teenager may have gone onto a life in the arts, inspiring others to follow their dreams despite facing obstacles.

Perhaps the soldiers gained a new perspective about their enemies and have been able to spread kindness to others who had been on opposite sides of the war.

The elderly man was able to reconnect with his family—I wonder, what wisdom was he able to impart to the four generations below him that might have otherwise been lost to history?

That's the ripple effect in action. Just like the ripples of a small pebble move outward and grow, acts of giving and kindness can spread and impact the lives of many others for generations to come.

As I stared out at the endless sea, fish making a snack of my feet, I realized that someone else's ripple effect had brought me to Sri Lanka in the first place. A viral video had inspired the concept of LSTN, and even though I didn't know the woman in the video—or the person who had made the video, or the one who had given her the hearing aid—I was carrying their impact forward and making it my own. Even when they were gone, they would live on through that ripple, just as I would through those touched by my experiences, and so forth.

This book has focused heavily on your life, but in the end, it's about way more. The richer you are in experiences, the more you have to give to others. The more joy, love, and wisdom you cultivate for yourself, the more you spread in the world. You become valuable to others when you share your experiences with them, thus creating opportunities for them to build their own experiential wealth.

When you're gone, the only thing that remains behind is what you've given to others. That's how you can live forever: through the impact you have on other people. In the end, serving others is the most powerful way to feel your life is well spent.

The Science of Giving

When we asked our survey participants what they thought the most valuable experience of their lives were, thousands replied with an example of giving back or helping others.

"My family took in refugees from Ukraine and it completely changed my perspective on life, the world, and the resilience of humanity." —Eric, Miami

"I volunteered as a Big Brother to a child here in Chicago for many years and was able to mentor him—now he has his own family and is a successful environmental lawyer!" —Tim, Chicago

"I train dogs for the blind and it's not only been the most fun and adorable experience but it makes me feel good that they're going on to help others." —Jesse, Raleigh

"My greatest memory was when I built a well in Ethiopia, to see the joy from the local people made me tear up and it made me feel like I had a real impact." —William, Boston

"I was an elementary school art teacher for 30 years and I loved helping kids discover their creativity and passions." —Mary, Cleveland

"When my sister passed away suddenly, I adopted her daughter and was able to help her have a fulfilling life, even though the circumstances were awful." —Joann, Boulder

"I worked as a park ranger in Yellowstone when I was younger, and I loved protecting Mother Earth and seeing the joy it brought the families who visited." —Bob, Big Sky

> "In college, I was able to stay in Nepal for free in exchange for teaching English to kids, and it was not only the most fun time of my life but also the most eye opening."
> —Kimberly, Atlanta

We weren't surprised—we've experienced the value of giving first hand, many times over. Maybe you have too. But until we did some research, we had no idea just how deeply giving can affect the giver.

You already know that serving others feels good. But that warm glow isn't in your imagination—it's actually measurable in your body. When you give to others, your brain releases all kinds of feel-good hormones (just like novel experiences, but apparently even more).[41] Giving is associated with lower stress and blood pressure, as well as less depression. One study found that seniors who volunteered tended to live longer, even after accounting for their age, health status, and lifestyle habits.[42]

On the emotional side, researchers consistently find that giving leads to greater happiness and satisfaction. One study published in the *Journal of Economic Psychology* found that people who spent money on others reported higher levels of happiness than those who spent money on themselves.[43] Another study published in the journal *BMC Public Health* found that people who volunteered had lower levels of depression and higher levels of well-being compared to those who didn't volunteer.[44] Furthermore, a study published in the journal *Emotion* found that people who performed acts of kindness for others experienced an increase in positive emotions and satisfaction, and a decrease in negative emotions.[45]

Forget about retail therapy—the fun of a new gadget or outfit fades shockingly fast, but the joy of giving to others sticks around.

It seems logical, but many religious, spiritual, and philosophical traditions teach that giving leads to prosperity, not the other way around. There's scientific evidence to support this idea. One study found that the act of giving appears to have a positive influence on income—not just a correlation but an actual causal effect.[46]

What's amazing is that this appears to be a universal feature of humanity. Experiments have shown that people all over the world, living in very different circumstances and cultures, feel the emotional benefits of helping others.[47] Even people who have little to give find happiness in sharing what they do have, as do those who have abundant resources. And while different cultures may take different views on the importance of the individual versus the community, that doesn't seem to change the fact that it simply feels good to help your fellow humans.

Everyone Has Something to Give

Life isn't fair.

I am reminded of this over and over on my travels. I've seen elephants in a nature preserve, with miles to roam, abundant resources to sustain them, and their families to love and protect them...and I've seen a lone elephant chained to a pole in the middle of the city with tourists poking at it and only a pail of dirty water to drink. I've met people with private planes at their disposal whenever they want to jet off to a tropical island...and I've met a boy who lost his legs and tied wooden planks to his forearms so he could crawl for miles just to get to our mission site for the chance to hear.

Some are lucky enough to be born into circumstances where they are safe, loved, and given plenty of opportunities. Many others are not, through no fault of their own. No matter where you fall on this spectrum, there will always be people more fortunate and less fortunate than you.

When we focus too much on those who have more, we can feel like we don't have enough. Our instinct is to hoard what's ours and tell ourselves, "I'll share when I have more. When I've paid off my debts and built up my savings, *then* I'll give to charity. When my schedule isn't so jam-packed, *then* I'll volunteer my time. When my needs are all met, *then* I can be generous to others." Sounds a lot like Someday Syndrome, doesn't it?

On the other hand, when we focus on lifting up those less fortunate than us, we realize how much we have to be thankful for. As the saying goes, "Somewhere, there is someone in a hospital bed praying and dreaming of what you are complaining about." Sometimes when I am stressed out rushing to get somewhere, I catch a glimpse of my feet and tear up as the memory of that boy and his wood planks comes flooding back. At times I can get down on myself for not doing or having enough, and memories like the elephant come to mind. Even on my worst days when I've felt like the world is ending, I can fill myself with gratitude and recognize the privileges that I have—health, clean water, access to sanitation, a roof over my head, freedom, and the fact that I woke up to another day.

Everyone, no matter their circumstances, has something to give—even if it's just a smile or a kind word.

I saw this clearly on a recent trip to India. After battling cows on Delhi freeways, waking up at 4 a.m. to be alone at the Taj Mahal, and meditating at Gandhi's ashram, I headed to Mumbai to meet with local education and water filtration nonprofits. There I learned that the massive city was roughly 60 percent slums—millions of people living in makeshift houses of corrugated metal sheets, tarpaulin, and scrap materials. Despite the efforts of government agencies and NGOs, access to basic amenities like clean water and sanitation remained limited. Residents faced many challenges, including inadequate infrastructure, high rates of crime and drug abuse, and limited healthcare and education. The area was also prone to flooding during the monsoon season, which made life even harder.

I had already seen extreme poverty in other parts of the world, and I admit I expected these slums to resemble some scenes of desperation and hopelessness I had witnessed before. Instead, I encountered the opposite—everyone around me seemed remarkably cheerful. Everywhere we walked, people smiled, waved, and said hello to us. Children giggled and played in the streets, and every corner was full of vibrant activity and community. I found the residents displayed incredible resilience, adaptability, and a very positive attitude toward life. It blew my mind how full of pure joy they were.

I asked my local friends how this could be true in the midst of such challenging circumstances, and the answer was simple: karma. Of course, everyone has heard of karma, but I had never actually seen it at the forefront of a culture like this. Nearly 80 percent of India is Hindu, and according to Hindu belief, every individual has an eternal soul that is reborn over and over. The nature of the body and the conditions of one's life in each reincarnation are determined by one's karma, which is the sum total of all one's actions, thoughts, and intentions in previous lives. Good actions lead to good karma, while bad actions lead to bad karma. Intention matters, too; good deeds only create good karma when performed with genuine good intentions, not selfish or deceitful ones.

The happiness I saw didn't justify or romanticize the challenges these people faced. But my takeaway from this experience is that even in these difficult living conditions, there was a palpable sense of generosity, kindness, and hope. They did the most with the least, not the least with the most like many of us do. They focused on what they could give, not what they lacked, and their quality of life was better for it—we can all learn from that.

When you show other people generosity and kindness, they immediately feel more inclined to do the same, not only to you but to everyone. It makes sense: when someone is kind to you, it lifts your spirits. It drains your stress and anger. It renews your belief in people. In that state of mind, you're much more likely to be benevolent to the next person you meet. In fact, just witnessing or hearing about someone else's kindness can have this effect, even if you weren't involved at all. This, in turn, strengthens the social fabric and fosters a sense of community.

So, what small acts of kindness can you display this week? Maybe you give a stranger a compliment, write a letter or email to someone who inspires you, or sit down with an elderly person and ask them about their life. You never know how this can inspire them to do the same for someone else. What goes around comes around.

Start With What Matters to You

You don't have to go on an international mission trip to make a positive impact on the world. There are plenty of opportunities to give, big and small, right where you are. So many, in fact, that it can be hard to figure out where to start.

My advice? Focus on what you care about. Don't worry about whether it's the most important or most urgent problem in the world. There are many, *many* different needs to fulfill, and trying to compare them and choose the most "deserving" is a colossal waste of time. What truly matters is how you feel about the problem you choose to tackle, because if you genuinely care, you'll stick with it. I had felt deeply connected to helping others hear because of my lifelong passion for music. It was rewarding and meaningful to me, so that connection motivated me to continue doing it, therefore making a bigger and more lasting impact in the end. Would I have done the same with a cause I didn't feel connected with? For short periods, maybe—but definitely not long term.

When our nonprofit was forced to stop doing mission trips in 2020, I felt like I had lost my purpose. Giving hearing on a global scale was on pause for who knew how long, and it created a hole inside me. I looked at my passions and skills and thought about other ways I could help others. That's when I started writing the stories for this book and asking the people around me how I could help them have the experiences in their lives that they really wanted. It gave me a sense of purpose and direction again.

Choosing how to give back isn't about who is more deserving or what's more important to society. Many people (and other living things and, of course, our planet) need help in many different ways, and the goal isn't to rank them. It's to find something that matters to you and *do it.*

Think about the issues that resonate with you on a personal level. Maybe you or someone you know has been personally affected by a particular struggle, such as hunger, mental health, or domestic violence. Maybe you empathize deeply with a certain group, like female entrepreneurs, refugees, or first-generation college students. Maybe you value certain things very highly, like ocean conservancy, special education, prison reform, or keeping art programs in schools. Maybe you care about a specific park, community farm, or historical building that holds a special place in your heart.

Start by focusing on one cause that feels like a top priority for you. Do a little research. What philanthropic organizations exist in that space? What problems are they focused on, and how do they try to solve them? What information can you find about the quality of the organization and the impact it has made?

Choose an organization whose work resonates with you, that you would be excited and proud to be involved with. If you can spare a few dollars, make a donation, but don't stop there.

Try to put your boots on the ground, where you can interact directly with the people or places you want to support. Go spend a few hours pitching in at the animal shelter, or the food bank, or the youth program—whatever cause you feel the need to contribute to. Make it a regular thing, and you'll start building relationships with the people you're serving and your fellow volunteers, making it even more fun and meaningful.

Go deeper and offer to contribute your special skills. Maybe you have the expertise to improve the organization's outreach efforts, update their website, plan or host an event, help with PR, or provide snacks for the volunteers. Most nonprofits operate on shoestring budgets, and any extra help (especially highly skilled help) is hugely appreciated. It doesn't have to feel like work. Maybe you and your friends love poker. You could organize a poker tournament for your chosen charity so you can have an impact while having fun and building relationships.

This kind of hands-on involvement is so much more powerful than just making a donation because it impacts *you*. You become emotionally invested in the work, which means you'll stick around, and your efforts will compound massively over time. You're also far more likely to spread the word and bring other supporters to the cause, which can multiply your impact many times over. Plus, it cultivates a spirit of empathy, generosity, and kindness that carries into everything else you do.

What Will Your Ripple Effect Be?

I stifled laughter as the tears rolled down my cheeks. I thought to myself, *This is either really selfish or really stupid, or both.*

We had lured a small group of friends and family to Joe's storage unit with chips and guacamole and a promise that we'd only take 45 minutes of their time. They stood in a semicircle facing our caskets. And when I say "caskets," I mean the long boxes Joe and I had cobbled together ourselves with $35 of plywood and nails from Home Depot. We printed headshots of ourselves and displayed them on a stand next to the box. One by one, they took turns speaking about us as if we were truly gone forever.

We weren't actually dead, of course. I'm not writing this from beyond the grave. We had just taken our "live like you're dying" philosophy a little too far this time.

This fake funeral isn't as crazy as it sounds. Well, maybe it is, since it's been parodied by *Curb Your Enthusiasm*, but we can't be blamed for inventing it. We first heard of this concept while on a press tour for LSTN's launch in Korea in 2014. A funeral company there had started offering free funeral services for the living, and tens of thousands of people have participated since then.[48] The idea is to help people appreciate life and contemplate their approach to it, before it's too late to make a change. It was such a popular "attraction" that we couldn't get in, so we did our own version upon returning from Seoul.

Imagining (and acting out) your own death in such detail may seem bizarre, but it's a powerful exercise. It makes you ask the tough questions: How will you be remembered? What will you leave on the Earth after you're gone? What's your legacy?

What struck me as I laid there sweating in the storage unit was that our friends and family didn't mention our (traditional) accomplishments. They talked about the impact we had inspired them to make in their own lives and for other people. They said things they had never told us before...like how we were the ones who had inspired them to start their own businesses with social impact. How they had hiked the Pacific Crest Trail after seeing us tackle Machu Picchu. How they had asked for help with their anxiety after seeing us push past our own fears.

These were *our* legacies. Our ripple effect.

The Final Countdown

To be honest, our fake funeral in the crowded storage room with the plywood boxes was not my ideal scenario, so I'm glad it was just the dry run. Family, take note.

I'd much rather put the "fun" back in "funeral" by throwing a party I would have liked to attend while living.

I want to share photos of all my favorite memories. Like the one with my sister and cousins as little kids giggling on Christmas Eve. The one of me and my mom on a road trip through the Rocky Mountains. The photo of me in the UK, my first hustle that opened a world of possibilities. The one of me as a teenager with a guitar, having no idea where that would eventually lead me. The one at a taco night in North Hollywood in my twenties with the friends who showed me what community meant. The one of Joe and me in Peru with the first person we ever saw hearing for the first time. The one of hunting with my dad. The photos of me in front of all seven Wonders of the World, in awe of what this amazing planet has to offer. And hopefully one of me celebrating the launch of this book, a lifelong dream come true.

I want my dog Taco to be the guest of honor, and for everyone to take a turn showering him with love and telling him he's been a very good boy (most of the time).

I want my Spotify funeral playlist blasting (opens with "Highway to Hell," crescendos with "Another One Bites the Dust," and ends with "The Final Countdown").

I want a friend to take a bouquet off the coffin and throw it into the crowd to see who is next.

I want it catered with my favorite foods—greasy Detroit-style pepperoni pizza, baked crab hand rolls from Katsuya, served with the "Love" natural wine I drank while living in Northern California.

I'm begging to not be put in a pantsuit in a coffin. I want to be dressed in my Ray Bans, leather jacket, Led Zeppelin shirt, ripped Levi's, and dinosaur slippers and sent off on my well-worn Almond surfboard into the Pacific in Malibu at sunset. Okay, that one *might* be illegal, so if you're trying to avoid prison, feel free to send my ashes off into the waves instead.

I want to have gift bags of swag handed out at the exit, like at the Oscars. But instead of fancy gadgets, I want them to contain the books that guided me through the ups and downs of my life, the vinyl records that shaped me when I was young, and the seashells and stones I collected outside my beach shack and on my travels around the world. The rest of my stuff can be sold to pay for all of the above. And someone should definitely take my airline miles and go somewhere they always wanted to go.

Afterwards, I want someone to take my phone and text everyone, "Thanks for coming! See you again soon!"

I want it to be a celebration of life, not a commiseration of death.

I want it to be an *experience*.

✦ ✦ ✦

EXERCISE

Imagine Your Ending

This exercise may feel a bit morbid, but it will bring you incredible clarity about what you need to do when you finish this book.

1. Take a few moments to imagine your funeral and write down the vision of what you want when that time comes. Who will be there? Where do you want it to be? What photos of your life will be on display? What music will play? What other details are important to you?

2. Share this vision with those closest to you. It may be a strange or uncomfortable conversation, but it will help them understand and support you.

3. Now you're going to write your own obituary—twice. For the first one, focus on your current life. What are the pivotal moments (good and bad) that define your life story? What will people remember about you when you're gone?

4. Now imagine your ideal life—your Treasure Map life. Write a new obituary based on that vision.

5. How big is the gap between your two obituaries? What choices can you make now to get you closer to the life you want? How can the tools in this book (like the Treasure Map) help you have the experiences you really want in life?

Note: All exercises in the book are available to download or print on our website, ExperientialBillionaire.com.

CONCLUSION

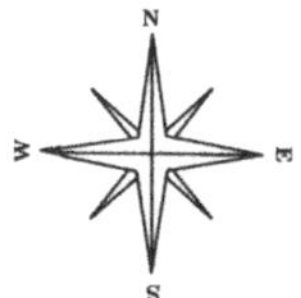

Joe:

If you want more proof that what you've learned here really does lead to a fulfilling, regret-free life, you're in luck, because I have one more story to share—one that unfolded as we wrote this book. It was the ultimate test of everything we believe, say, and do.

My wife, Yasmine, is from the tiny island of Bahrain in the Middle East. (It's okay, look it up if you have to—she's used to it.) She went to college at Chapman University in Southern California, and we met when she was visiting some old college friends in Los Angeles. She was living in London at the time, so right from the start, we had to be very deliberate about making the most of our limited time together.

Thankfully, we both loved to travel, so we took every opportunity to make our visits into memorable trips. Our first Christmas together, we backpacked through Thailand. The following summer, we slept under the stars for a week at a wakeboard camp on a remote lake in Córdoba, Spain. The next year we went to the Arctic Circle, where we stayed in traditional tents, chased the northern lights, and went ice fishing over the New Year's holiday.

When we got married, we did the same, uniting our families and friends (who lived on opposite sides of the planet) in one incredible place: Bali. It was a dream come true. We spent three weeks in paradise, the first ten days with all our friends and family and then another ten days exploring on our own, hiking volcanoes, riding motorbikes through rice paddies to remote beaches, taking boats to tiny islands without cars or electricity at night, and, of course, surfing.

Then, we spent our first year as a married couple traveling the globe and working remotely. I had spent a decade hoarding all my American Express credit card points, and I was ready to put them to use. We wanted to start a family, but first, we wanted to explore all the places we might consider living long term, as well as visit some destinations from our bucket list. So, we chose a few places for longer stays of a month or more (London, Paris, and New York), then wove in many smaller trips, some for fun and others for work or philanthropic missions with LSTN.

The result was an incredible year of fun, growth, and learning in Utah, London, Nairobi, Rwanda, Paris, Hamburg, Tahiti, New York, Athens, Mykonos, Tuscany, Hong Kong, China, Tokyo, Bahrain, Dubai, and Bangkok. (I'll be honest, I had to look at the Google doc we sent our parents to remember all the places we went.)

While we were traveling, we spent a lot of time discussing what we wanted our future to look like, and the Treasure Map exercise showed us the way, time and time again. Starting a family was at the top of the list, assuming we would be fortunate to have children. But we still wanted to explore living in different places and spend some time near our families. So, we made a plan. We would have our first child in London and our second in Los Angeles, and when the youngest was around two years old we would go live abroad somewhere for a full year—probably Bali, for its great quality of life and low cost of living.

Over the next five years, our Treasure Map kept our priorities in focus. We traveled as much as we could, we filled up our life in LA with tons of new experiences, and we were incredibly blessed to start our family pretty much as planned. Our first son was born in London in October 2019 and our second in LA in March 2022, right as we were in the middle of writing this book.

Life was good.

A few months later, our three-month-old son stopped breastfeeding from my wife's right breast. He violently refused to take milk from that side, no matter how much she encouraged him. The breast became swollen and painful, but she attributed it to a blocked milk duct, something that had happened with our older son when he was around the same age. After a week of trying to clear the milk duct at home, we randomly ran into our doctor at the grocery store, and he encouraged her to get it checked out to be safe. That was on a typical Sunday afternoon.

My wife was sure it was nothing to worry about. She was too young. Her 34th birthday was just a week away. She was fit, rarely drank, didn't smoke, and was completely healthy otherwise. But she agreed to see the doctor on Monday, just to be safe. That was followed by an ultrasound on Tuesday, a mammogram on Thursday, and a biopsy on Friday.

The following Thursday afternoon, four days after her birthday, we returned to the breast center. The nurse practitioner braced us as gently as she could before telling us that the "can't happen to us" had just happened. My wife had breast cancer—and it was very aggressive.

It felt like our whole world had collapsed.

A CT scan, a PET scan, an MRI, and bone scans would be scheduled within days. Chemotherapy and immunotherapy would start immediately after that. The rest of the plan would be figured out once we had more information.

A week later, we received her test results and final diagnosis: stage 3, triple negative, regionally metastasized breast cancer with six tumors, growing at a rate of 67 percent. Translation: It was growing fast and had already spread to the lymph nodes around her breast. Genetic testing came back positive for the BRCA-1 mutation, which causes a high risk of breast, cervical, and ovarian cancer. That night, I just sat in our kids' room and cried while my wife showered and the boys slept.

In the blink of an eye, everything can change. Bridget and I had already finished the first draft of the book, making it seem so surreal and ironic that we were being given this harsh reminder of exactly what we are trying to teach you. Life is short and uncertain.

The next eight months were grueling. My wife went through chemotherapy, immunotherapy, and a double mastectomy. A week after the surgery, her pathology report came back stating that there were no longer signs of cancer in the breast tissue that was removed. The treatments had worked. She was cancer free.

It's hard to describe the weight that was lifted at that moment. Even knowing she still had to do six more months of immunotherapy and five weeks of radiation to minimize the possibility of recurrence, suddenly we could breathe again. She was now officially a cancer survivor, and we were working to make sure it never came back. I cried more that day than on the day she was diagnosed. Her courage and resilience throughout her journey was nothing short of remarkable.

We had a close call with death, just like my dad did. But unlike him, we didn't come out the other side with a desire to start life fresh and do things differently—we didn't have to. We were already following our Treasure Maps. Our priorities and plans remain the same. If anything has changed, it is only how we have grown in strength, grace, and appreciation for each day. We are savoring every precious moment—the little things, like smiles and giggles from our kids, and the bigger things that we look forward to on our horizon.

If things had gone the other way, of course we all would have been devastated with immeasurable heartache and grief—but not regret. We had done the work. When we look back at the decade we've spent together, it feels like we've filled up every minute with meaningful experiences. We didn't waste a moment.

As we look to the future, we're planning with the intention and urgency of those who know that life is short, so it's important to enjoy the ride. No matter how much money you make, at the end, you'll be willing to give it all away for just one more day. Time is your currency, and experiences are the greatest wealth of life.

In the end, that's the only wealth that matters.

ACKNOWLEDGEMENTS

The following people were instrumental in helping us get through the (many) hurdles and challenges we faced to make this dream of ours a reality. We are forever grateful for your support and love.

JOE

My cancer-beating superhero wife, Yasmine Alsairafi: you make this adventure called life so much better every single day. I love you to the moon and back.

My in-laws, Jaffer and Debbie Alsairafi: you've shown me what it means to show up and give everything. I'm profoundly grateful for all the help you've provided us and forever inspired by your selfless dedication to your family.

The rest of the Alsairafi family, Sarah, Sammy, Mariam and Talal: Best. In-laws. Ever.

My family, Ginny (mom) and Bryan Horstman; my brothers, James and Mike, and their families; and Paul Huff (cousins for life): thanks for the unconditional love, making me laugh, and putting up with me all these years.

Couldn't have made it this far without you—Darren and Lulu Crawford, Dan and Karen Ellerman, Maddie and Sonny Sinclair, Wilmer and Amanda Valderrama, Jared and Jonalyn Nixon, and Rob Nand: your presence in my life is an absolute blessing. Thank you for always being there to share the best of times, catch me when I fall, and lift me back up.

BRIDGET

My family, Lori, Terry, Cassie, Katheryn, Matt, Judy, Don, Harold, Tammy, Kristen, Donelle, Kyle, Keith, Max, Nicole, Ann, Jason, Kenny, Colton, Evan, Cam, July, Taco, Mary, Jack, and Sally: thank you for giving me my love of nature and adventure, the ability to laugh at literally anything all the time, and unconditional love.

My squids, Rachel Connors, Liz Rockmore, Joe Demin, Dan Dworkis, and Vlad Gyster: thank you for supporting me through the creation and completion of this book and giving me incredible community through an extremely difficult time in my life.

My framily, Blaire Nichols, James Lockwood, Jocelyn Maynes, Bryan Grone, Neeraj Sharma, Melissa Sanchez, Kenny Czadzeck, Bob McIntosh, Aaron Glassman, Sarah Horton, Matt Connors, and Sergio Zaldivar: thank you for growing up with me through the last two decades in Los Angeles. I wouldn't be who I am without our experiences together.

Hoffman Institute, Drew Horning, Amy Thompson, Barbara Burke, Liz Severin, and everyone else I met through this incredible organization: thank you for giving me freedom.

Everyone at Universal Music Group and Warner Music Group, especially Michael Lawson and Lloyd Hummel: thanks for giving me a unique education and letting me achieve my childhood dreams.

The entire Reality/Schusterman and JDC community: thank you for including me.

BOTH OF US

LSTN—Zoya Biglary, Max Fronek, Lauren Nipper, Molly Leighton, Matt Lauer, Bryan Mead, Jon Rappaport, Tyler White, Pete Delgrosso, and Brady Forseth: thank you for being by our side through all the blood, sweat, and tears at LSTN. Building something from nothing that created such a huge ripple effect would not have been possible without you.

Bill and Tani Austin and the entire Starkey Hearing Foundation family: thanks for showing us what true purpose looks like.

Josh Linkner, Sara Smith, Pete Sheahan, Ryan Estis, Seth Mattison, Jenny DeRosse, Connor Trombley, Ivy Gustafson, and the entire ImpactEleven staff and community: thank you for being our advisors, professional safe space, and friends on this journey.

Jeff Rosenthal, Elliott Bisnow, Brett Leve, and the incredible Summit community: thanks for the experiences and friendships over the years.

To our extended family and those who gave us crucial feedback during this process: Ben Nemtin, Brittany Hodak, Alex Banayan, Tero Isokauppila, Caitlin Crosby, Jake Strom, Adam Bornstein, Adam IN-Q Schmalholz, Nina Ojeda, Faten and James Stewart, Peter Kim, Andrew Pollard, Kostas and Mia Morfis, Brian and Cris Nolan, Zach Mendelsohn, Scott Bailey, Chad Penry, Dave Lingwood, Sean Macgillivray, Daymond John, Jaspar Weir, Kevin Hekmat, Freddie Prinze and Sarah Gellar, Jeremy Taylor, Christian Bendixen, Serinda Swan, Chari Cuthbert, Chris Noyes, Duncan Penn, Penni Thow, Cris Judd, Andrea Lake, Steve Titus, Isaac Horne, Dave Hosford, Eric Anthony, Conrad Jackson, Deirdre Maloney, Frankie Delgado, Scott Budnick, Bryan Macgillivray, Tadao Salima, Claire Harper, Ross Asdourian, Brian and Kamilla Wayne, Alix Traeger, Arezu Hashemi, Alexa Brandt, Julia Taylor-Brown, Sanjay and Rachel Amin, Kelly Balch, Zach Glassman, Jessica Encell, Smiley Poswolsky, Jesse Israel, Jason Goldberg, Rachel Sheerin, Jordan Tarver, Frankie Russo, Chris Schembra, Matthew Emerzian, Clay Hebert, Naren Aryal, Justin Wren, Joey Aviles, Erin Stafford, Sterling Hawkins, Cara Forney, Jeff Johnson, Shawn Bagazinski, Steve Osika, Cory Popovich, Kim Dunham, Kristin Meek, Anastasia Tchaplyghine, Harriet Linklater, Ashley Edes, Jobi Manson, Marlena Marchewka, Joe Valle, Kevin Conroy Smith, Ki Walker, Maurice Martin, Mike De La Rocha, Mike Dyer, Rob Badgely, Ryan Westberg, Tyler Christopher, Alyaa and Ali Karimi, Tara and Salim Hakim, Mazin and Selma Almardhi, Yousif and Sarah Alawi, Zeid and Reem Baitaineh,

Faisal and Zeina Bataineh, Ali Fakhro, Beatriz Posada, Salman and Amelda Alzayani, Lamia and Turk, Shaikha Fakhro, Latifa Shakar, Ranjan Goswami, Andrew Bardsley, Chloe Swycher, Anne-Charlotte Dhoste, Bob Taylor, William Drewry, Jeff Stibel, Kevin and Rick Yorn, Bill Choi, Amanda Dykema, Tom Creed, Helen Krause, Elliot Fuhr, Nu Dao, Meghan Shank, Ericka Turnbull, Patricia Galea, Chris and Cassidy Cole, Madison Fitzpatrick, Alix Steinberg, Donnie McLohon, Kelly Teemer, and Macy Robison.

There are many more who have supported, held us up, and kept us going that we surely have missed in this section of acknowledgments. Please accept our deepest apologies along with our deepest gratitude for being in our lives.

And finally, to our readers, listeners, and partners: we have loved books longer than we could read and this was a huge honor to create one. Thanks for your faith in us. We hope this inspires you to live a life rich in meaningful experiences.

NOTES

1 Shai Davidai and Thomas Gilovich, "The Ideal Road Not Taken: The Self-Discrepancies Involved in People's Most Enduring Regrets," *Emotion* 18, no. 3 (April 2018): 439–52, https://doi.org/10.1037/emo0000326.

2 Bronnie Ware, *The Top Five Regrets of the Dying: A Life Transformed by the Dearly Departing*, rev. ed. (Carlsbad, CA: Hay House, 2019).

3 Andrew Wilt, *Age of Agility: The New Tools for Career Success* (Seattle: Sustainable Evolution Inc., 2017).

4 Anji Connell, "Feast for the Senses: Experiencing the Positive Effects of Travel at Home," *Home Journal*, April 29, 2020, https://www.homejournal.com/en/article/Feast-for-The-Senses%3A-Experiencing-the-Positive-Effects-of-Travel-at-Home/.

5 Tess Gregory, Ted Nettelbeck, and Carlene Wilson, "Openness to Experience, Intelligence, and Successful Ageing," *Personality and Individual Differences* 48, no. 8 (June 2010): 895–99, https://doi.org/10.1016/j.paid.2010.02.017.

6 "Global Health Estimates: Life Expectancy and Leading Causes of Death and Disability," World Health Organization, https://www.who.int/data/gho/data/themes/mortality-and-global-health-estimates.

7 "People spend 'half their waking hours daydreaming,'" *BBC News*, November 12, 2010, https://www.bbc.com/news/

health-11741350. After gathering 250,000 survey results, the Harvard team concluded that this group of people spent 46.9% of their time awake with their minds wandering.

8 Michael Bernard Beckwith, *Life Visioning: A Transformative Process for Activating Your Unique Gifts and Highest Potential* (Boulder: Sounds True, 2012).

9 Lucia Capacchione, *Visioning: Ten Steps to Designing the Life of Your Dreams* (New York: Jeremy T. Parcher/Putnam, 2000).

10 Shakti Gawain, *Creative Visualization: Use the Power of Your Imagination to Create What You Want in Your Life* (Novato, CA: New World Library, 1995).

11 Bronnie Ware, *The Top Five Regrets of the Dying: A Life Transformed by the Dearly Departing*, rev. ed. (Carlsbad, CA: Hay House, 2019).

12 David Hamilton, "Does Your Brain Distinguish Real from Imaginary?" October 30, 2014, https://drdavidhamilton.com/does-your-brain-distinguish-real-from-imaginary/.

13 Andrew Huberman, "Dr. Emily Balcetis: Tools for Setting & Achieving Goals," August 1, 2022, *Huberman Lab* podcast, https://hubermanlab.com/dr-emily-balcetis-tools-for-setting-and-achieving-goals/.

14 Jory Mackay, "The Myth of Multitasking: The Ultimate Guide to Getting More Done by Doing Less," *RescueTime* (blog), January 17, 2019, https://blog.rescuetime.com/multitasking/.

15 Fiona MacDonald, "Science Says That Technology Is Speeding Up Our Brains' Perception of Time," *ScienceAlert*, November 19, 2015, https://www.sciencealert.com/research-suggests-that-technology-is-speeding-up-our-perception-of-time.

16 Clay Johnson, interview by Scott Simon, *Weekend Edition Saturday*, NPR, January 14, 2012, https://www.npr.org/2012/01/14/145101748/is-it-time-for-you-to-go-on-an-information-diet.

17 Dan Buettner, Finding Happiness at Work, *Psychology Today*, February 21, 2011, https://www.psychologytoday.com/us/blog/thrive/201102/finding-happiness-work.

18 Rachel Feintzeig, "How to Become a Better, Braver Public Speaker," *The Wall Street Journal*, October 17, 2022, https://www.wsj.com/articles/how-to-get-your-public-speaking-mojo-back-11665867795.

19 Marcel Schwantes, "Science Says 92 Percent of People Don't Achieve Their Goals. Here's How the Other 8 Percent Do," *Inc.*, July 26, 2016, https://www.inc.com/marcel-schwantes/science-says-92-percent-of-people-dont-achieve-goals-heres-how-the-other-8-perce.html.

20 Peter M. Gollwitzer and Lucas Keller, "Mindset Theory," in *Encyclopedia of Personality and Individual Differences*, ed. Virgil Zeigler-Hill and Todd K. Shackelford (Cham, Switzerland: Springer, 2016), 1–8, https://doi.org/10.1007/978-3-319-28099-8_1141-1.

21 Sarah Milne, Sheina Orbell, and Paschal Sheeran, "Combining Motivational and Volitional Interventions to Promote Exercise Participation: Protection Motivation Theory and Implementation Intentions," *British Journal of Health Psychology* 7, no. 2 (May 2002): 163–84, https://doi.org/10.1348/135910702169420.

22 Joel Falconer, "How to Use Parkinson's Law to Get More Done in Less Time," *LifeHack* (blog), March 17, 2023, https://www.lifehack.org/articles/featured/how-to-use-parkinsons-law-to-your-advantage.html.

23 Based on our own Life Experience Survey.

24 Barrett Wissman, "An Accountability Partner Makes You Vastly More Likely to Succeed," *Entrepreneur*, March 20, 2018, https://www.entrepreneur.com/leadership/an-accountability-partner-makes-you-vastly-more-likely-to/310062.

25 Leon Ho, "How to Find an Accountability Partner to Help You Build Habits," *LifeHack* (blog), February 14, 2023, https://www.lifehack.org/862621/accountability-partner.

26 Stephen Newland, "The Power of Accountability," *The Standard Newsletter* (blog), *AFCPE*, 2018, https://www.afcpe.org/news-and-publications/the-standard/2018-3/the-power-of-accountability/.

27 See the work of Joseph Campbell for more on the idea of the hero's journey.

28 Neringa Antanaityte, "How to Effortlessly Have More Positive Thoughts," TLEX Institute, https://tlexmindmatters.com/how-to-effortlessly-have-more-positive-thoughts/.

29 Gabriella Paiella, "The Brain-Changing Magic of New Experiences," *GQ*, May 27, 2021, https://www.gq.com/story/brain-changing-magic-new-experiences.

30 Julie Beck, "When Nostalgia Was a Disease," *The Atlantic*, August 14, 2013, https://www.theatlantic.com/health/archive/2013/08/when-nostalgia-was-a-disease/278648/.

31 Arthur C. Brooks, "Nostalgia Is a Shield Against Unhappiness," *The Atlantic*, March 9, 2023, https://www.theatlantic.com/family/archive/2023/03/nostalgia-defense-unhappiness-happy-memories/673320/.

32 Liz Mineo, "Good Genes Are Nice, but Joy Is Better," *The Harvard Gazette*, April 11, 2017, https://news.harvard.edu/gazette/story/2017/04/over-nearly-80-years-harvard-study-has-been-showing-how-to-live-a-healthy-and-happy-life/.

33 Andrew Huberman, "Time Perception & Entrainment by Dopamine, Serotonin & Hormones," November 15, 2021, *Huberman Lab* podcast, https://hubermanlab.com/time-perception-and-entrainment-by-dopamine-serotonin-and-hormones.

34 Alyson Krueger, "Getting by With a Little Help Finding Friends," *The New York Times*, June 3, 2021, https://www.nytimes.com/2021/06/03/style/friends-apps-bumble-soho-house.html.

35 Alok Patel and Stephanie Plowman, "The Increasing Importance of a Best Friend at Work," *Gallup*, August 17, 2022, https://www.gallup.com/workplace/397058/increasing-importance-best-friend-work.aspx.

36 Stuart Brown, "Play Is More Than Just Fun," TED video, 2008, 26:21, https://ted.com/talks/stuart_brown_play_is_more_than_just_fun.

37 Stuart Brown and Christopher Vaughan, *Play: How it Shapes the Brain, Opens the Imagination, and Invigorates the Soul* (New York: Penguin Group, 2009).

38 Jessica Stillman, "Having a Hobby Is More Important Than Ever," *Inc*, May 14, 2020, https://www.inc.com/jessica-stillman/having-a-hobby-is-more-important-than-ever.html.

39 Theo Dawson, "Learning, Emotion, and the Goldilocks Zone," *Medium*, March 10, 2019, https://theo-dawson.medium.com/learning-emotion-and-the-goldilocks-zone-30295765dd7a.

40 Andrew Huberman, "How to Learn Skills Faster," May 17, 2021, *Huberman Lab* podcast, https://hubermanlab.com/how-to-learn-skills-faster/.

41 Arthur C. Brooks, "How to Buy Happiness," *The Atlantic*, April 15, 2021, https://www.theatlantic.com/family/archive/2021/04/money-income-buy-happiness/618601/.

42 "Why Giving Is Good for Your Heart," Cleveland Clinic, December 7, 2022, https://health.clevelandclinic.org/why-giving-is-good-for-your-health/.

43 Tamás Hajdu and Gábor Hajdu, "The Association Between Experiential and Material Expenditures and Subjective Well-Being: New Evidence from Hungarian Survey Data," *Journal of Economic Psychology* 62 (October 2017): 72–86, https://doi.org/10.1016/j.joep.2017.06.009.

44 Jerf W. K. Yeung, Zhuoni Zhang, and Tae Yeun Kim, "Volunteering and Health Benefits in General Adults: Cumulative Effects and Forms," *BMC Public Health* 18, no. 8 (July 2017), table 2, https://bmcpublichealth.biomedcentral.com/articles/10.1186/s12889-017-4561-8/tables/2.

45 S. Katherine Nelson et al., "Do Unto Others or Treat Yourself? The Effects of Prosocial and Self-Focused Behavior on Psychological Flourishing," *Emotion* 16, no. 6 (September 2016): 850–61, https://doi.org/10.1037/emo0000178.

46 Arthur C. Brooks, "Does Giving Make Us Prosperous?" *Journal of Economics and Finance* 31 (September 2007): 403–11, https://doi.org/10.1007/BF02885730.

47 Lara B. Aknin et al., "Prosocial Spending and Well-Being: Cross-Cultural Evidence for a Psychological Universal," *Journal of*

Personality and Social Psychology 104, vol. 4 (April 2013): 635–52, https://doi.org/10.1037/a0031578.

48 Daewoung Kim and Youngseo Choi, "Dying for a Better Life: South Koreans Fake Their Funerals for Life Lessons, *Reuters*, November 5, 2019, https://www.reuters.com/article/us-southkorea-livingfunerals/dying-for-a-better-life-south-koreans-fake-their-funerals-for-life-lessons-idUSKBN1XG038.

Made in the USA
Las Vegas, NV
27 October 2023

79774436R00184